ITALIAN
STILL LIFE PAINTINGS
from Three Centuries

John T. Spike

Centro Di
National Academy of Design
Old Masters Exhibition Society of New York

National Academy of Design, New York
February 2 - March 13, 1983

Philbrook Art Center, Tulsa, Oklahoma
April 9 - June 30

Dayton Art Institute, Dayton, Ohio
July 30 - September 11

Copyright 1983 Centro Di
Text copyright © 1982 John T. Spike
Centro Di cat. 157
ISBN 88 7038 055 6
Library of Congress Catalog Card Number 82-6204

Printed in Italy by Stiav, Florence 1983
Layout by Centro Di, Florence
Text Editor, Michele K. Spike

This project is supported by a grant from the
National Endowment for the Arts.

The exhibition was organized by the National Academy of Design and the Old Masters Exhibition Society of New York, in association with the International Exhibitions Foundation. The exhibition is being circulated by the International Exhibitions Foundation.

Honorary Patron for the Exhibition
His Excellency, Rinaldo Petrignani
Ambassador of Italy to the United States

Executive Committee
Old Masters Exhibition Society of New York

John H. Dobkin
Marco Grassi
Robert L. Manning
D. Stephen Pepper
John T. Spike
Ann Sutherland Harris

Advisory Council
Old Masters Exhibition Society of New York

Italo Faldi
Egbert Haverkamp-Begemann
Terence Hodgkinson
Paul Horgan
Denis Mahon
Konrad Oberhuber
Alfonso E. Pérez Sánchez
Erich Schleier
Malcolm R. Waddingham
Ellis K. Waterhouse

Advisory Committee for the Exhibition

Carlo Bertelli
Raffaello Causa
Marco Chiarini
Andrea Emiliani
Italo Faldi
Oreste Ferrari

Lenders to the Exhibition

Bergamo, Accademia Carrara
Campione d'Italia, Silvano Lodi Collection
England, Private Collection
Faenza, Pinacoteca Comunale
Florence, Galleria degli Uffizi
Florence, Palazzo Pitti
Hartford, Wadsworth Atheneum
London, Matthiesen Fine Art Limited
Los Angeles, Los Angeles County Museum of Art
Lugano, Baron H. H. Thyssen-Bornemisza Collection
Milan, Pinacoteca di Brera
Modena, Galleria Estense
Montreal, Private Collection
Naples, Museo Nazionale della Certosa di S. Martino
Naples, Museo Nazionale di Capodimonte
Naples, Museo Duca di Martina
Naples, Novelli Collection
Naples, Pagano Collection
New York, Private Collection
Providence, Museum of Art, Rhode Island School of Design
Rome, Galleria Borghese
Sarasota, John and Mable Ringling Museum of Art
Washington, D.C., National Gallery of Art

Contents

Italian Still Life Painting from Three Centuries is the inaugural effort of a group called the Old Masters Exhibition Society of New York. This informal association was conceived more than three years ago and has met irregularly at the National Academy of Design since then. Its purpose is the organization of selective exhibitions that focus on important European traditions in the fine arts. The works to be exhibited would be limited in number, would be of the highest quality, and would introduce a provocative subject or theme to the American public.

Exhibitions of this nature, while quite common to European museums and galleries, are rarely seen on these shores. OMESNY hopes with this and other exhibitions to add a certain diversity to the artistic offerings in this country.

The current exhibition seems to us to fulfill OMESNY's aims. First, works in the exhibition number 46. Second, they represent the best available examples of Italian still life painting, and for this we are in debt to the museums and individuals who have so generously lent to the exhibition. And third, they introduce a subject that is little known in America and one that only in recent decades has gained attention in Italy.

The aims of OMESNY mesh very neatly with those of the National Academy of Design. Founded in 1825 in New York, the National Academy, aside from its important annual juried exhibition, has over the years housed ground breaking exhibitions of European Art. One example is the Durand-Ruel exhibition in 1886 that introduced French Impressionism to America. So it is fitting that the National Academy of Design join with OMESNY in offering *Italian Still Life Painting from Three Centuries*.

An international exhibition of this magnitude can only come into being through the good-will and efforts of many persons. We are especially grateful to have had the guidance of the distinguished scholars who served as the Advisory Committee for the exhibition: Prof. Carlo Bertelli, Prof. Raffaello Causa, Prof. Marco Chiarini, Prof. Andrea Emiliani, Prof. Italo Faldi, and Prof. Oreste Ferrari. We should like also to express our gratitude for the patronage of His Excellency, Rinaldo Petrignani the Ambassador of Italy to the United States and the assistance of On. Vincenzo Scotti, Ministro dei Beni Culturali, Minister Sergio Romano, Ministero degli Affari Esteri Dr. Guglielmo B. Triches, Ministero dei Beni Culturali, also to Dr. Piergiuseppe Bozzetti, Italian Cultural Attaché in Washington, D.C., and Dr. Marco Miele, former Director of the Italian Cultural Institute in New York, for their liaison with the Italian Embassy.

The list of Lenders to the Exhibition enumerates the participation of museums and private collectors in many cities and countries: to each we owe a profound debt of gratitude. It is our hope that the success of this magnificent exhibition will repay their expression of support for this important cultural exchange.

During the preparation of this exhibition, I have been in constant correspondence with museum colleagues in Italy and in the United States, whose invaluable cooperation deserves acknowledgement (with apologies for any inadvertent omission): Prof. Dante Bernini, Prof. Luciano Berti, Mr. J. Carter Brown, Dr. Jean Cadogan, Dr. Caterina Caneva, Avv. Filippo Capece Minutolo, Mons. Eugene Clark, Prof. Michele D'Elia, Bishop Giovanni Fallani, Prof. Mazzino Fossi, Mons. Angelo Paredi, Sir John Pope-Hennessy, Dr. Franklin W. Robinson, Dr. Francesco Rossi, Prof. Nicola Spinosa, Dr. Sara Staccioli, Dr. William H. Wilson.

For this inaugural effort, the Old Masters Exhibition Society of New York is particularly fortunate to have as Guest Curator the noted scholar John T. Spike. Dr. Spike's great knowledge of Italian painting and his devotion to the exhibition have been its key ingredients. To Dr. Spike goes our gratitude for a most able job.

John H. Dobkin
Director, National Academy of Design

During the past two years, it has been my privilege to represent the National Academy of Design as Guest Curator, and it has been a pleasure for me to meet and correspond with the many persons whose efforts have made possible *Italian Still Life Paintings from Three Centuries*. First of all, I would like to express my gratitude to each of the Lenders to the Exhibition, private collectors and public institutions. I hope very much that this selection of paintings and these catalogue essays will convey the enthusiasm and enlightenment that I took away from my many discussions of Italian still lifes with the participants in this exhibition.

This exhibition has been organized under the joint auspices of the National Academy of Design and the Old Masters Exhibition Society of New York. I am deeply grateful to the members of the OMESNY for their encouragement, assistance, and patience throughout this long journey. In particular, John H. Dobkin, Director of the National Academy, and Marco Grassi devoted themselves unstintingly to this project; no one could ask for more able or more congenial colleagues.

The same commitment to this exhibition and to the importance of its theme was demonstrated by the distinguished scholars who comprised the Advisory Committee for this exhibition: Prof. Carlo Bertelli, Soprintendente per i Beni Artistici e Storici, Milan; Prof. Raffaello Causa, Soprintendente per i Beni Artistici e Storici della Campania; Prof. Marco Chiarini, Direttore della Galleria Palatina, Florence; Prof. Andrea Emiliani, Soprintendente per i Beni Artistici e Storici delle province di Bologna, Ferrara, Forlì e Ravenna; Prof. Italo Faldi, Rome; Prof. Oreste Ferrari, Rome. These professors contributed their time, energy, and expert knowledge to this undertaking from its inception, and were instrumental in its realization. Drawing upon his lifelong study of Italian still life paintings, Prof. Causa offered invaluable guidance regarding the proper format for this exhibition.

For consultation, photographs, and similar assistance, I would also like to thank: Avv. Giorgio Alpeggiani, Prof. Giuliano Briganti, Mr. Domenico De Conciliis, Mrs. Cynthia Clark, Mr. Piero Corsini, Mr. Alfredo de Palchi, Dr. Tilman Falk, Dr. Craig Felton, Mr. Lawrence Fleischman, Roberto and Sandra Franceschini, Mr. Claudio Gasparrini, Contessa Anna Grandi, Prof. Mina Gregori, Dr. Sheldon Grossman (who first suggested the theme of this exhibition), Mrs. Rudolf J. Heinemann, Dr. Frima Fox Hofrichter, Mr. Ian Kennedy, Avv. Fabrizio Lemme, Mr. Timothy Llewellyn, Mr. Silvano Lodi, Dr. Gianfranco Malafarina, Dr. Suzanne Folds McCullagh, Mr. Bruno Meissner, Dr. Manuela B. Mena Marqués, Dr. Otto Naumann, Prof. Konrad Oberhuber, Dr. Wolfgang Prohaska, Mr. William W. Robinson, Mr. Nelson Shanks, Prof. Eduard Safarik, Dr. Scott Shaeffer, Prof. Seymour Slive, Dr. Beppe Somaini, Prof. Nicola Spinosa (for many valuable communications), Dr. Timothy Standring, Dr. Ann Sutherland Harris, Dr. Franca Varignana, Prof. Lamberto Vitali, Mrs. Virginia Wageman, Prof. Federico Zeri.

The technical arrangements for the exhibition have been the responsibility of the International Exhibitions Foundation, Washington, D.C., under the direction of Mrs. John A. Pope. I thank Miss Taffy Swandby, Administrative Director, for her considerable efforts in this regard. The enthusiastic response of the Philbrook Art Center in Tulsa, Oklahoma, and the Dayton Art Institute, which museums agreed to sponsor the tour of this exhibition, was of course a most welcome development.

My researches for the catalogue were undertaken at the Witt Library, Courtauld Institute, London; the Frick Art Reference Library, the Watson Library of the Metropolitan Museum of Art, and the Public Library, New York; and the Bibliotheca Hertziana, Rome. To these excellent facilities and their staffs, I am grateful. It is written that the last shall be first: I therefore conclude these acknowledgements with reference to my foremost debt of gratitude, which is that owed to my beloved wife, Michele. Assistant in my researches, editor of this catalogue, partner-in-life, she is forever an inspiration.

J.T.S.

The great age of still life painting in Italy, as in Holland, Flanders, Spain and France, occurred during the seventeenth century, the Age of the Baroque. Of these different schools, the Dutch, Flemish, and Spanish masters of still life have been justly celebrated in numerous exhibitions and publications in many languages. The reputation of French still life painting prior to the nineteenth century has naturally benefited from the long shadow cast by the singular personality of Jean Siméon Chardin (1699-1779). By contrast, the Italian tradition of *natura morta*, or still life, has not found a place in American public collections, and still lifes are rarely mentioned in general surveys of Italian art. Most admirers of European painting would be surprised to learn that Italy produced a still life specialist — Evaristo Baschenis — of comparable genius to Chardin. This exhibition of *Italian Still Life Paintings from Three Centuries* is in fact the first ever presented in America on this theme; its catalogue is the first study of Italian still lifes to appear in English, except for the relevant pages in the translated editions of Charles Sterling's fundamental *Still Life Painting*.

It is the purpose and privilege of this exhibition to introduce to American audiences the Italian genius for the depiction of *natura in posa* ("nature suspended"). The selection of paintings has been restricted to forty-six outstanding examples, many of which bear easily the label of "masterpiece". These forty-six paintings are not presented as a comprehensive survey of the countless numbers of still lifes painted in Italy from the sixteenth through the eighteenth centuries. The variety and abundance of the Italian still life tradition were amply demonstrated in the monumental exhibition, *La Natura Morta Italiana*, of 1964/65 (Naples, Zurich, Rotterdam), in which 306 works from these three centuries were exhibited. The objective of the present exhibition is to identify the most gifted masters in that tradition, among whom, besides Baschenis, there are several artists of international stature: namely Fede Galizia, Giuseppe Recco, Giovan Battista Ruoppolo, and Arcangelo Resani.

Two other criteria were applied to this compilation of *Italian Still Life Paintings from Three Centuries*. With very few exceptions, the artists represented herein were specialists in the genre of still life: these are the personalities that have been the most neglected by scholarship. Certain artists who made their contemporary reputations as figure painters, such as Fede Galizia, Panfilo Nuvolone, and Jacopo Chimenti, called Empoli, have been included nevertheless in recognition of the prominence (not necessarily numerical) of still lifes in their *oeuvres*. The second criterion was the resolution to omit an artist, notwithstanding his merits, if a suitable example could not be found. Thanks to the enthusiastic response of the lending museums and private collectors, every still life specialist of the first rank is worthily represented in this exhibition excepting only Pietro Paolo Bonzi and Mario Nuzzi, called Mario dei Fiori — both artists by whom documented works are exceedingly rare.

The paintings on exhibition have been ordered in this catalogue with reference to their regional schools of origin and to their dates. The schools of Lombardy, Rome, Naples and Florence have therefore been divided in order to respect the successive generations of artists represented in this show. Lombardy, due to the activity of Vincenzo Campi in Cremona, is generally held to have been the cradle of still life painting in Italy. The pair of paintings by Vincenzo Campi (Exh. nos. 1 and 2) are the earliest works — datable to the 1580's — in this exhibition. Campi's works are not properly still lifes because they depict scenes that are defined by the actions of the figures; however, the artist's concern to differentiate between the sundry kinds of fruits, fish, game, and so forth, evinces a naturalistic bias that anticipates the first Italian painters of still lifes [1].

The origins of still life painting in Europe are the subject of scholarly controversy; however, it is clear that the painting of independent still lifes, mostly flowerpieces at first, became widespread in Europe during the last decade of the sixteenth century. As the crossroads of the Renaissance, Italy figured importantly in the exchange of ideas amongst the earliest proponents of this new genre of painting. Scholars differ significantly in their views as to the course of events leading up to this moment and as regards the nature of the interchange, if any, between North European and Italian artists during the "pre-history" of the genre prior to the 1590's.

In his text, *Still Life Painting from Antiquity to the Twentieth Century*, Charles Sterling has compiled an impressive mass of evidence to demonstrate that most, if not all, of the archetypical motifs of European still lifes (bowls of fruit, vases of water, skulls, etc.) were commonly depicted in Hellenistic and Roman paintings (now lost), mosaics, and wall frescoes [2]. Sterling argues that the still life schemata that were invented in antiquity were rediscovered following the Middle Ages by Italian artists of the fourteenth century, who were influenced both by the surviving artifacts of classical Rome and by the descriptions in the writings of Pliny the Elder of the still life and genre paintings of the ancient Greeks.

Sterling's thesis is supported by several considerations. In the first place, the art of antiquity was much more accessible to the artists of the Early Renaissance than we might imagine from our present perspective, since so many of the ancient ruins in Rome and elsewhere in Italy were destroyed as a result of the urban renewal policies of the sixteenth and seventeenth centuries. In addition, Pliny's anecdotes regarding the illusionistic paintings of Zeuxis and the "low" subject matter of the Hellenistic artist, Piraikos, were constantly repeated in the art criticism of the Renaissance and the Baroque. For Sterling, the illusionistic, or *trompe l'oeil*, qualities of the decorations of antiquity constituted their most immediate attraction for Renaissance artists: the Eucharistic vessels painted by Taddeo Gaddi in *trompe l'oeil* niches in the Baroncelli Chapel of S. Croce, Florence, ca. 1337-38, are cited as central examples in this phenomenon at its outset. Similar motifs of objects on shelves in open niches or cabinets became the standard subject matter of wood-inlay, or *intarsia*, decorations in Italy after the middle of the fifteenth century. In particular, Sterling is surely right to detect the inspiration of antiquity in the *trompe l'oeil* marquetry commissioned by Duke Federico Montefeltro of Urbino for his *studiolo*, ca. 1476. The significance of such designs in wood marquetry for the subsequent painting of independent still life subjects is established in the view of Sterling and of Ingvar Bergström, the leading historian of Dutch still lifes, by the *trompe l'oeil* character of the earliest such composition, the famous *Partridge and Mail Gauntlets* (Alte Pinakothek, Munich) signed and dated 1504 by Jacopo de' Barbari. A Venetian painter in the service of the Elector of Saxony, de' Barbari was also influenced by the watercolor studies of Dürer and Lucas Cranach, as Bergström has pointed out[3].

In the studies by Bergström and most recently by Sam Segal, the independence of the Netherlandish tradition of still life painting has been stressed[4]. These scholars doubt that antique motifs played a determinant role for Northern artists; they prefer to trace the genesis of still life painting in the Low Countries to the naturalistic vision of Jan van Eyck and Rogier Van der Weyden in the mid-fifteenth century and to the marked attention devoted to fruits, flowers, and insects in the borders of Early Renaissance manuscript illuminations, most notably in the work of the Master of Mary of Burgundy, ca. 1470. Indeed, Northern Europe has been the source of every independent still life painting from the early sixteenth century that has been rediscovered to date. The earliest flowerpiece that has yet come to light is a still life of lilies in a maiolica vase painted by Hans Memling, ca. 1490, on the reverse of a male portrait now in the Thyssen-Bornemisza collection; the picture represents an allegorical allusion to the purity of the Virgin[5]. The motif of the vase of flowers was employed throughout the sixteenth century as the bearer of symbolic meanings associated with the myriad varieties of flowers. The Westphalian artist, Ludger tom Ring the Younger painted three independent compositions of flower vases, a pair dated 1562 and a third from 1565[6].

There exists fragmentary evidence, mainly literary, which suggests that random instances of still life painting were occurring simultaneously in Italy. Charles Sterling strongly suspects that independent compositions of flowers in vases were painted by Giovanni da Udine during the first half of the sixteenth century. Giovanni was the highly esteemed still life specialist in the Roman workshop of Raphael; although his biographer, Giorgio Vasari, does not refer to easel paintings by Giovanni da Udine, he does mention a *trastullo* or notebook of studies by him and praises his painting of " every natural thing " (*tutte le cose naturali*). See the extended discussion of this issue in the entry for Exh. no. 7.

In his review of the first English edition (1959) of Sterling's *Still Life Painting*, Ernst Gombrich contributed evidence in confirmation of Sterling's thesis that the Italian Renaissance, ca. 1500, witnessed considerable progress towards the invention of independent still lifes[7]. Most importantly, Gombrich pointed to a document which appears to indicate that Antonio da Crevalcore, a Bolognese artist who is only known today through a few religious compositions, also painted still lifes. In a letter written in 1506 from Bologna to Isabella d'Este in Mantua, Girolamo Casio writes that he is sending her some olives, a painting of the *Magdalen* by Lorenzo di Credi, and a " painting full of fruit made by Antonio da Crevalcore, quite unique in this skill, but it seems to us here that he takes rather longer than nature does "[8]. Indeed, some scattered references to Crevalcore's interest in natural subjects can be found in other early sources; Filotto Achillini in his *Viridario*, 1504, compares him to Zeuxis of antiquity, whose paintings of grapes deceived the birds[9]; Antonio di Paolo Masini, *Perlustrata Bologna*, 1666, reports that " Antonio da Crevalcore of the house of Leonelli was a musician and a celebrated painter of flowers, fruits, and animals, which are seen with his name inscribed below; he was active in 1490 ".

If Giovanni da Udine and Antonio da Crevalcore painted independent compositions of flowers and fruits — which remains to be established — their still lifes would represent the culmination of the striving for naturalism which largely characterized Italian painting during the fifteenth century. Flowers, fruits, and animals were painted with increasing abundance and vivacity in the altarpieces and portraits of the Early Renaissance under the impetus of a highly developed language of symbolism. This practice reached singular heights in the paintings of Carlo Crivelli, a Venetian, both for the care with which the artist individualized the fruits and for the prominence afforded to them. A similar *Madonna and Child* by Crivelli to that illustrated here (R.P. 1) of ca. 1473 was the subject of exegesis by M. Levi D'Ancona in that author's authoritative study on horticultural symbolism in Renaissance painting.

These naturalistic tendencies continued in North Italy even after the passing of the High Renaissance, ca. 1520, when the treatmen of fruits and flowers as attributes in religious images or fresco decorations in Rome and Florence became more generalized[10]. Roberto Longhi perspicaciously observed that certain passages in the art of Moretto da Brescia, most notably the basin of fruit at the base of that artist's *Madonna and Child Enthroned with Saints* altarpiece of ca. 1540-45 in S. Andrea, Bergamo (pl. 2), must have served as prototypes for still lifes by Caravaggio and other Lombards (cf. Exh. nos. 3 and 4). The dal Ponte family in Bassano and Venice were propagators of another vital current of naturalism. By 1561, Jacopo Bassano was already noted (by Vasari) as adept in the painting of " little things " (*cose piccole*), which can be understood as a reference to still life elements[11]. Together with his sons, Francesco and Leandro, Jacopo Bassano painted genre scenes or allegories, such as the Seasons of the Year that lent themselves to the depiction of every kind of material object. We illustrate here an *Allegory of the Element of Fire* (Liechtenstein Collection, Vaduz), signed by Francesco Bassano and datable to ca. 1580 (pl. 5). These inventions by the Bassanos appear to have been independent from the slightly earlier paintings by Pieter Aertsen in the 1550's of market scenes and butcher shops. It is well known that the works of Aertsen and of his pupil Joachim Beuckelaer, which made their way very quickly into Italian collections, were direct influences on the analogous compositions of Vincenzo Campi (Exh. nos. 1 and 2).

The early sources make reference to one other Italian pioneer of seeming importance. Although no paintings by Carlo Antonio Procaccini (born ca. 1550) have as yet been identified, his fame as a painter of still lifes survived well into the seventeenth century, when his biography was compiled by C. C. Malvasia (1678). Procaccini was the son of an artist and the younger brother of Camillo and the elder of Giulio Cesare Procaccini, both of whom became figure painters of renown after the family moved from Bologna to Milan, about 1585. According to Malvasia, Carlo Antonio resolved to surpass his brothers in the genres of landscape and still life painting. In the latter field, Malvasia informs us, there was hardly a private house in Milan which did not have some piece by him of " fruit and flowers... portrayed so naturally that everyone was charmed by them ". Many were sent to Madrid for the Royal Collection, but these paintings likewise await rediscovery. In addition to his importance as one of the first Italian specialists in still life, Carlo Antonio Procaccini quite possibly played a major role in the early development of Spanish still life painting.

Pl. 1. Michelangelo da Caravaggio, Basket of Fruit, *31x47 cm, Pinacoteca Ambrosiana, Milan.*

In a brief but influential article of 1950, Roberto Longhi advanced a radically new perspective on Italian still life painting, rejecting the possibilities that it was either an inheritance from antiquity (Sterling) or a relatively late development dependent upon Netherlandish precedents (Bergström and Segal). Although couched in historical terms, Longhi's distinctions partake liberally of aesthetic observances. Longhi distinguished between two principal currents in the history of European still life painting. Into one category, by far the largest, Longhi placed those painters whose purposes in still life subjects were confined to either "descriptive sedulity, or the presumptions of herbalists and provincial scientists, or the display of diligent technique"[12]. In short, these are still lifes that were conceived for decorative or illustrative purposes solely. The entire production of still lifes in the sixteenth century prior to Michelangelo da Caravaggio (i.e. the paintings by North Europeans) was also placed by Longhi into this category. For Longhi, these scattered antecedents — he specifies only the "strange figure-puzzle compositions of Arcimboldi and the useless microscopes of the Flemings" — pertain to the sixteenth-century fascination for curiosities and rarities such as were collected in *Wunderkammer*. The religious symbolism that is present in most of these early still lifes tests the arbitrariness of this definition: Longhi's response was to term this accomodation of technical finesse and mystical content a "superior hybrid". Fede Galizia is named as characteristic of this half-zone of artistry.

In contradistinction to this body of painters, who conceived of still lifes as a "speciality" and therefore limited field of art, Longhi credited Caravaggio on the basis of the famous *Basket of Fruit* in the Ambrosiana, Milan, of ca. 1596 (pl. 1) with the invention of "modern painting" and a conception of still life which broke sharply from sixteenth-century antecedents and contemporaries, including Jan Brueghel the Elder. He associated Caravaggio, moreover, with a distinguished line of spiritual successors:

Pl. 2. Alessandro Buonvicino, called Moretto da Brescia, Detail from Madonna and Child enthroned with Saints, *S. Andrea, Bergamo.*

Baschenis, G. M. Crespi, Chardin, Goya, Courbet and Manet. Common to each of these artists is the conviction that the simplest objects, acutely observed, possess potentialities of expression that transcend the narrow preconceptions of the still life genre. It is a modern attitude, as Longhi pointed out, to allow that still lifes or any other aspect of daily existence have the same applicability to art as the " major genres " of sacred or historical painting. In the famous dictum reported ca. 1620 by the marchese Vincenzo Giustiniani to the effect that " Caravaggio said that it cost him as much effort to make a good painting of flowers as of figures " [13], Longhi found support for his thesis that Caravaggio was the first painter to refute the hierarchy of the genres. Anti-academic convictions can likewise be detected in Caravaggio's statement in 1603 that the best artists are those who know how " to paint well and to imitate well natural things " [14]. This remark must have exasperated his contemporaries, who were steeped in late sixteenth-century notions of the divine origins of artistic inspiration; simple " imitation " was despised as an activity suitable for apes, not artists. Although Caravaggio's empirical approach to nature became one of the foundations of seventeenth-century painting, winning countless adherents among painters in Italy and abroad during the first three decades of the century, it failed to make any (favorable) impression whatsoever upon the artistic theory of the time. In any event, it was Roberto Longhi's intention to demonstrate, in Sterling's words, that Caravaggio's still life "marks the birth of the modern still life, definitively stripped of religious or intellectual allusions and ranked on an equal footing with the human figure " [15].

On a more specific level, it has been proposed by Raffaello Causa that the Ambrosiana *Basket of Fruit* must be considered the first " pure " still life painted in the Italian tradition [16]. Following Longhi, Causa asserts that the diverse " pre-history " of still life antecedents was irrelevant to Caravaggio. Only the naturalistic

biases of Caravaggio's native Lombardy are admitted as pertinent to his process of invention. Unlike Longhi, Causa recognizes the influence that certain sixteen-century precursors of still life painting had on subsequent painters if not Caravaggio himself; Vincenzo Campi in Cremona and Bartolomeo Passarotti in Bologna are cited in this regard. Causa acknowledges, moreover, the constant " pressure " that North European still life painters exerted on the Italian school at every stage of its development. The prolific schools of the Low Countries are considered by Causa to be separate and vital traditions which were responsive to their native cultural impulses: this constitutes a more reasonable view of the superb paintings of Georg Hoefnagel, Georg Flegel and Jan Brueghel *de Velours* than their characterization by Longhi as the " patient labors of nuns and Carthusians ".

As articulated by Raffaello Causa, and supported most recently by Carlo Volpe [17], the proposal to identify Caravaggio as the inventor of Italian still life painting has taken a prominent position within the controversy concerning the origins of still life painting in Europe. By linking the names of Galileo and Caravaggio, Volpe has invoked the issue of *zeitgeist* in support of Longhi's thesis, since the spirit of objective inquiry which infused Caravaggio was coincidentally the critical innovation in science in the early seventeenth century. It may be mentioned in this context that landscape painting, which also emerged as an independent genre during this period, was the creation of artists who increasingly referred to the actual forms of nature as opposed to their imaginations. Anna Ottani Cavina has suggested that Adam Elsheimer, one of the most influential landscape painters in Rome during the first decade of the century, represented in the nocturnal sky of his *Flight into Egypt* of ca. 1610 the Milky Way and other astronomical features lately discovered by Galileo [18].

The history of Italian still life painting after the turn of the seventeenth century has been succinctly told by Charles Sterling. Rather than recapitulate Sterling's outline, this Introduction will confine itself to the aspects of the Italian school that are represented in this exhibition. The scope of this discussion will be augmented somewhat by the appended Reference Photographs. For detailed analysis of individual artists the reader is referred to the relevant entries.

The subsequent development of Lombard still lifes after Vincenzo Campi (Exh. nos. 1 and 2) is traced by four paintings from the early seventeenth century: an anonymous pair (Exh. nos. 3 and 4) and works by Fede Galizia (Exh. no. 5) and Panfilo Nuvolone (Exh. no. 6). Most likely under the influence of Flemish painters, such as Georg Hoefnagel (1542-1600) and Jan Brueghel the Elder (" Velvet Brueghel ") (1568-1625), Lombard still lifes typically isolate their subjects on the center of the pictorial stage. The earliest known example appears to be a *Still Life with Peaches on a Plate* (Lorenzelli Collection, Bergamo) (fig. 6) by Ambrogio Figino (1548-1608), which has been dated ca. 1595, i.e., contemporaneous with Caravaggio's *Basket of Fruit* [19]. Longhi preferred a slightly later date for the Figino. The first securely dated still life of the Lombard school is a work of 1602 by Fede Galizia, formerly in the Anholt Collection, Amsterdam. Caravaggio's Lombard roots are, of course, manifest in the Ambrosiana picture.

At mid-century, still life painting in Lombardy again came into prominence following some decades of decline and its consequent clipse by the Roman school with the activity of an extraordinary painter-priest, Evaristo Baschenis of Bergamo (Exh. nos. 22-25). Although not strictly a follower of Caravaggio, Baschenis represents a resurgence of a Caravaggesque faith in naturalism. The subject matter of Baschenis's still lifes of musical instruments brings to mind works of the contemporary Dutch school, but they could equally have been inspired by passages in genre paintings by Caravaggio and his followers; the earlier master's *Amor Victorious* in Berlin has often been cited in this context. During Baschenis's lifetime and for generations thereafter, Bergamo became the center of a mass production of still lifes in his manner. Bartolomeo Bettera (born 1639) (R.P. 10 and 11), the most talented pupil of Baschenis, promulgated a decorative, Late Baroque version of this style throughout the second half of the seventeenth century.

The early production of still lifes in Lombardy and Rome is linked by the career of Caravaggio. After 1592, when Caravaggio transferred to Rome from Milan, the young Lombard began his career (no earlier works are known) as a painter of single-figure scenes in which fruits and other still life articles are featured — and described with a startling specificity. Vincenzo Campi, Pieter Aertsen (1508/9-1575) (R.P. 2), and Bartolomeo Passarotti (1529-1592) in Bologna (R.P. 4), for example, had depicted the organic swellings and creases of natural things before Caravaggio; it was Caravaggio's inspiration to portray the every imperfection of the actual fruits on the table before him. Soon after his arrival in Rome, Caravaggio was employed for some months in the studio of Giuseppe Cesari, Il Cavalier d'Arpino (1568-1640) who was then the most promising star on the Roman horizon. Although condemned in the history books as a holdover from the late Maniera, d'Arpino deserves more credit than he has received for preparing the ground for the naturalistic renovations of Caravaggio and Annibale Carracci. As the principal designer of the vast fresco programs executed in the pilgrimage churches of Rome, especially St. John in the Lateran, in preparation for the Jubilee Year of 1600, Il Cavalier d'Arpino revived on a grand scale the Raphael school practice of framing figural scenes with pendulous festoons of luscious fruits and leaves. For this purpose d'Arpino employed teams of artists who specialized in fruit and flower motifs [20].

Of the six examples (Exh. nos. 8-15) in this exhibition from the Roman school of the early seventeenth century, two are paintings by Tommaso Salini, the first follower of Caravaggio in this genre who has been identified, the other four still lifes have all been at one time or are currently attributed to Caravaggio himself. The only still life of unquestioned authorship by Caravaggio is the Ambrosiana *Basket of Fruit* which picture was considered too precious to be sent abroad for exhibition. The profound impression made by Caravaggio qualifies him as the founder of the Roman school of still life, but the diversity of that school must always be borne in mind. The presence in Rome of artists from Northern Europe contributed greatly to the production in the new genres of landscape and still life. Although only landscapes from this period of the 1590's by Jan Brueghel *de Velours* are known, it cannot be irrelevant that this future master of the flowerpiece arrived in Italy ca. 1589, visited Naples in 1590, and was active in Rome 1592-94 and Milan 1595-96 prior to his return to Antwerp. Brueghel's first flower painting of secure date, the *Vase of Flowers*,

Pl. 3. Jacopo Ligozzi, Ramo di iberis e francolino, 62.5x45.7 cm, tempera on paper, Gabinetto Disegni Stampe degli Uffizi, Florence.

1606, in the Ambrosiana, was made for Cardinal Federico Borromeo, who apparently acquired Caravaggio's *Basket of Fruit* at about the same time. The motif of flowers in a glass vase was made famous by Caravaggio, whose mastery of the device was praised by Baglione and Bellori, and became almost immediately characteristic of the Roman school (see Exh. nos. 8, 9, 10, 11). On the other hand, Giovanni Baglione, who knew these artists personally, gave credit to Tommaso Salini for the invention of this motif. In the same article of 1950 that has been cited above, Roberto Longhi put forward a convincing reconstruction of the first reaction by Roman artists to the advent of Caravaggio. Based on a careful reading of Baglione's text, Longhi identified a "triumvirate" of Tommaso Salini, Pietro Paolo Bonzi, called Il Gobbo dei Frutti (or dei Carracci) (R.P. 13) and Giovanni Battista Crescenzi. Baglione actually describes an academy in the house of Crescenzi which encouraged artists to draw and paint still lifes from nature. At the time of Longhi's study no certain works by any of these three artists had been identified. In the three intervening decades, after some false steps, several still lifes have been convincingly attributed to Salini. Two signed works by P. P. Bonzi (ca. 1576-1636) have been traced but otherwise it has been difficult for scholars to augment his still life *oeuvre*. Bonzi's activity as a painter of fresco ornaments, as in the Palazzo Mattei 1618-24, and of landscapes with small figures is rather better known. In fact it is on the basis of similarities in the style of the figures that this writer is inclined to attribute to Bonzi a remarkable *Still Life with Fantastic Vase* (present whereabouts unknown) (R.P. 14) that epitomizes the vigor with which still life subjects were addressed by the pioneers in Rome. The reconstruction of G. B. Crescenzi's career as a painter — he was also an architect and a diplomat — is currently the focus of scholarly investigation, the results of which have not as yet been published.

The resilience of an archaistic mode of still life, that is, a style which emulated the sculpted vases and other classical motifs favored by sixteenth-century artists, is represented in this exhibition by a *Vase of Flowers* (Exh. no. 7) based on a design painted by Polidoro da Caravaggio on the facade of the Palazzo Milesi, Rome, ca. 1527. Agostino Verrocchi was the foremost practitioner in Rome of this nostalgic style (R.P. 53). From the archival researches of M. Gregori, Verrocchi's Roman activity has been documented from 1619 to 1636, a later period than the severity of his still lifes might have suggested[21].

The strictly Caravaggesque current in Roman still life painting seems not to have lasted past ca. 1620 before its character became diluted by two disparate tendencies: the Flemish sensibility for exquisiteness and the general shift in taste towards the energetic compositions of Baroque style[22]. Even Tommaso Salini appears to have bowed to the influence of Frans Snyders (1579-1657), who visited Rome before 1609 (cf. Exh. no. 13).

Michelangelo Cerquozzi (1602-1660), an important transitional figure, was among the first painters to inject Baroque dynamism into an essentially Caravaggesque outlook. We illustrate here a major example by Cerquozzi, previously unpublished, a *Cincinnatus Called from Retirement*, which is signed *MC* in the tangles of some vines (R.P. 20). The subject ingeniously satisfies both the contemporary taste for psychological narrative and the still life painter's involvement with the gifts of the harvest. Cerquozzi probably deserves credit for the relocation of still life subjects out-of-doors, but it was Michele Pace, called Michelangelo da Campidoglio (1610-1670), who was responsible for the more important development of integrating his still life subjects with atmospheric and lush landscape settings (R.P. 34 and 35). Unfortunately, no signed still lifes by Campidoglio have been recovered; attributions to this master have been made on the basis of comparison with a pair of paintings in the Hermitage, Leningrad, which were referred to this artist during the eighteenth century. Abraham Brueghel (Exh. no. 34) (R.P. 16) was the most perceptive of the plentiful followers of Campidoglio.

The other protagonists of Roman High Baroque still life painting were Mario Nuzzi (1603-1673), a flower specialist as his sobriquet, Mario dei Fiori, indicates (R.P. 31, 32, 33) and the enigmatic Francesco Fieravino, called Il Maltese (active ca. 1640-1660). The nephew and pupil of Tommaso Salini, Mario Nuzzi invented a dramatic and scintillating style of brightly-colored flower decorations. The exquisite garlands painted by Daniel Seghers (1590-1661), a pupil of Jan Brueghel the Elder who visited Rome in 1625-27, were crucial influences on Nuzzi. It was the latter's chief innovation to arrange his blooms with splendid profusion. Nuzzi frequently collaborated with the leading figure painters of the day, a practice of specialization that was probably also inspired by Flemish examples (cf. R.P. 6). Until that time, the tradition established by Campi and Passarotti and continued by Caravaggio, Cerquozzi, and Tommaso Salini (Exh. no. 12) had called for the painter to execute both figure and still life. With Carlo Maratti, the leading painter in Rome during the second half of the seventeenth century, Mario Nuzzi decorated the towering mirrors in the Gallery of the Palazzo Colonna, ca. 1660, with putti and grand vases of flowers (pl. 4). Prestigious commissions of this sort brought international fame to Mario dei Fiori, but typified the irreversable descent of the still life genre into the realm of decoration, down from the heights foreseen by Caravaggio.

Mario Nuzzi's counterpart in the painting of still lifes of precious objects in sumptuous interiors was Francesco Fieravino (R.P. 24 and 25). See the entry under Exh. no. 31 by Giuseppe Recco for an account of the influence of Fieravino's style, which was transmitted as widely as Nuzzi's. Notwithstanding his success, almost nothing is known of the training and travels of Il Maltese, not even whether he was in fact a native of Malta. His lavish style left its mark not only in Rome and on Giuseppe Recco in Naples, but also on Cittadini in Bologna, Bettera in Bergamo, and Meiffren Conte and others in France, where Maltese may even have visited. The Late Baroque still life painting of Rome became practically the exclusive province of gifted foreigners such as Christian Berentz (1658-1722), Franz Werner von Tamm (1658-1724) and Karel Vogelaer, called Carlo dei Fiori (1643-1695), not to mention Abraham Brueghel (Exh. no. 34). These artists propagated the decorative outlines established by Mario Nuzzi and Michelangelo da Campidoglio, but with noticeably less vigor. The most accomplished native son on the scene was Giovanni Paolo Spadino. A fine *Still Life with Melons* (Exh. no. 39) is here proposed as an early work by the artist, comparable to Campidoglio. By 1703, in which year Spadino signed and dated a still life in the Capitoline Museum, Rome (fig. 32), Roman still life painting had evolved into a truly international style common to foreign artists and Italian painters alike. As late as 1743 when he signed and dated a still life with putti and flowers (R.P. 48), Ignaz Stern (1680-1748) was working in this same tradition essentially unmodified.

Still life painting in the southern school of Naples seems not to have been prevalent earlier than perhaps ca. 1620. The eighteenth-century historian Bernardo De Dominici mentions Ambrosiello Faro and some other early painters of still life whose works have as yet resisted identification. Raffaello Causa has successfully compiled a corpus of paintings by Giacomo Recco (1603-ante 1653), who also belonged to this first generation of still life specialists in Naples, and who was the first of a distinguished family of artists[23]. Giacomo Recco painted flowerpieces in the "archaic" style, noticeably cognizant of Flemish precursors, as well.

Caravaggesque still life found a sympathetic shelter in Naples. The author of the masterpiece of Caravaggesque still life painting in Naples remains anonymous; R. Causa has dubbed this figure the "Master of Palazzo San Gervasio" in reference to the town near Matera where the canvas is preserved (R.P. 30)[24]. Formerly ttributed to the young Paolo Porpora, with whose style there are efinite links, the Palazzo San Gervasio *Still Life with a Dove in Flight* represents a finely wrought balance between the impressive solation of Caravaggesque naturalism and the unifying movement of the incipient Baroque. In style, the picture is therefore comparable to a Roman counterpart of the 1620's in this exhibition, attributed to the "Pensionante del Saraceni" (Exh. no. 1). The four paintings by Luca Forte in this exhibition reveal the fidelity of the Neapolitan interpretation of Caravaggio ca. 1630 as well as the reluctance with which Forte, one of the founders of the school, assimilated the Baroque tendencies subsequently imported from Rome.

ased on the solid foundation of the careers of Giacomo Recco, Luca Forte, and the anonymous Master of Palazzo San Gervasio, he still life painters of Naples constituted a cohesive and vital chool from the 1640's through the end of the century. It is interesting to note that the uncompromising naturalism of the figure paintings of Caravaggio and Jusepe de Ribera — which truck an immediate response in Neapolitan taste — survived undiluted in the local still lifes well after the figure painting of Naples had succumbed to the idealized qualities of Bolognese/Roman style. Neapolitan masters of still life had the apacity to assimilate foreign influences without sacrificing their ative character. For example, Paolo Porpora (Exh. nos. 27 and 28) was able to adapt the *sottobosco* subject matter of the Netherlanders Otto Marseus von Schrieck (1619-1678) and Matthias Withoos (1627-1703) into an animistic and quintessentially Neapolitan conception of nature.

orpora relocated in 1654 to Rome, thus leaving the field in Naples open to the competition of two great rivals, Giovan Battista Ruoppolo and Giuseppe Recco. Each of these was the utstanding member of a family of still life specialists. Giuseppe Recco was the pupil of Giacomo, his father; Giovanni Battista Recco (1615?-1660?) seems to have been the uncle of Giuseppe nd the chief proponent in Naples of a Spanish brand of still life [25]. signed *Basket of Lobsters*, previously unpublished, is illustrated mong the Reference Photographs (R.P. 38). Giuseppe Recco was himself the father of a large family, including Nicola Maria (R.P. 44) and Elena Recco, both of whom painted marine still lifes. The Ruoppolo faction included, among its many followers, Giuseppe Ruoppolo († 1710), the nephew of Giovan Battista (R.P. 46). In his exhibition, G. B. Ruoppolo, the master renowned for his exuberant compositions of fruit (Exh. no. 29), is also represented by a masterly *Still Life with Crab and Fish* (Exh. no. 30). For centuries the marine still lifes of Naples have been associated with the name of Giuseppe Recco. Of unusual historical interest and artistic merit is the *Marine Still Life with Fisherman* (Exh. no. 33), which is signed and dated by Recco but executed in collaboration with Luca Giordano. The prestige of Recco must indeed have been great (he was eventually knighted) for Giordano, who was caposcuola among Neapolitan figure painters, to have agreed to a secondary role [26].

he arrival of Abraham Brueghel in 1675, roughly, in Naples roved to be decisive for the subsequent development of the local chool, which had previously resisted the intrusion of the Flemish/Roman conceptions of decorative still life. The legacy of Caravaggio had continued to manifest itself even within the Baroque parameters of the styles of G. B. Ruoppolo and Giuseppe

Pl. 4. Mario Nuzzi, called Mario dei Fiori (figures by Carlo Maratti), Mirror Painted with a Vase of Flowers and Putti, 248x166 cm, Palazzo Colonna, Rome.

Recco. In the works of these masters, in contrast to Abraham Brueghel's, the viewer is sensible of thematic content, above all a distinctively Neapolitan awe and dread before the copiousness of nature. Andrea Belvedere was alone amongst the Neapolitan still life painters at the end of the seventeenth century in his adherence to the peculiar character of Neapolitan style, although eventually even he incorporated the fanciful effects associated with the Roman school. Baldassare De Caro (1689-1750) (R.P. 22) and Gaetano Cusati († ca. 1720) (R.P. 21) deserve mention as adroit followers of Abraham Brueghel. An exhaustive treatment of the whole panorama of Neapolitan still life painting is available in the monograph by Raffaello Causa (1972).

In marked contrast to its importance as the center of a classical style of figure painting, and probably because of this theoretical bias, Bologna did not produce a major school of still life painting. At the end of the sixteenth century, the naturalistic experiments of Passarotti and Annibale Carracci in their paintings of butcher shops and peasants at meal would seemingly have promised

Pl. 5. F. Bassano, The Element of Fire, *145x187 cm, Liechtenstein Collection, Vaduz.*

otherwise. Paolo Antonio Barbieri (1603-1649) (R.P. 7), the brother of the famous Giovanni Francesco Barbieri, called Il Guercino, was notably active in nearby Cento prior to his early death in 1649. At mid-century the field was left to a pair of transplanted Milanese painters, P. F. Cittadini (Exh. no. 26) and his much less gifted brother, Carlo. Following studies in Rome during the 1640's, the Cittadini imported to Bologna a decorative High Baroque style indebted to Il Maltese. Working until 1732 in relative isolation in Parma, Felice Boselli (Exh. no. 36) (R.P. 15) managed nevertheless to experiment in his prolific *oeuvre* with nearly every mode of still life that had yet been introduced in Italy. The highest achievements in this genre by a Bolognese artist were undoubtedly the pair of still lifes painted at Livorno in 1708 by G. M. Crespi for Grand Prince Ferdinando de' Medici.
The Florentine school of still life traces its origins to the natural science illustrations made in great numbers by Jacopo Ligozzi (1547-1626), who was called to Florence ca. 1576 by Francesco I de' Medici, Grand Duke of Tuscany (pl. 3, R.P. 5). Similar qualities of formal clarity and crisp outline characterize the still lifes painted by Jacopo Chimenti, called Empoli (Exh. no. 18) during the early 1620's. Ligozzi's tempera paintings on paper exerted an even more immediate influence on Giovanna Garzoni, a much younger artist, who was native to Ascoli Piceno in the Marches but must have trained in Florence (Exh. nos. 19, 20, 21). Born in 1600, Giovanna Garzoni reaped the benefits of still life patronage which was by this time present throughout Italy; she worked for the most distinguished collectors in Venice, Florence, Rome, Naples, and Turin. The activity of Simone del Tintore (R.P. 49, 50), a pupil of Pietro Paolini, established Lucca as a mid-century refuge for Caravaggesque still lifes.
The close of the seventeenth century coincided with the end of the great epoch of Italian still life painting; under the sponsorship of the Medici court however, Florence remained a receptive market for fine still lifes through the first decades of the eighteenth

century. The schools of Rome and Naples were quantitatively productive in this period, but only Florence may be said to have sponsored a new development, namely the sudden enthusiasm for *trompe l'oeil* subjects (cf. R.P. 29). In the selection for this exhibition the diversity of the Florentine school early in the eighteenth century is well represented by paintings by Bartolomeo Bimbi, Cristoforo Munari and Nicola Van Houbraken (the last being native to Messina, the son of a Flemish pupil of Rubens). Munari was active in both Florence and Rome; he was trained in the latter place and was there exposed to the works of Christian Berentz, a German master of considerable fame.
Still lifes did not achieve distinction in either Genoa or Venice. An interesting self-portrait by Giacomo da Castello (active ca. 1660-1680), showing the painter at his easel, is illustrated amongst the Reference Photographs in this catalogue (R.P. 19), but no Venetian example was selected for this exhibition.
Margherita Caffi (R.P. 17 and 18) is described in contemporary sources as *veneziana*, but she was mainly active as a flower painter in Lombardy. In Genoa, which was in most aspects of art a satellite of Antwerp during the seventeenth century, the Flemish preference for sacred or mythological subjects *cum* still life (e.g. *Noah and the Animals Entering the Ark*, the *Voyage of Jacob*) was observed. Giovanni Agostino Cassana (ca. 1658-1720) painted animal pictures of some vivacity, but documented works by the artist are rare. Only one Genoese still life is included in the present selection. Happily it is the acknowledged masterpiece of the school, *The Larder* by Anton Maria Vassallo (Exh. no. 35), a painting which was once attributed to Velázquez.
As noted above, the eighteenth-century still life paintings in this Exhibition have been selected for the most part from the Florentine school. Apart from these, Arcangelo Resani (Exh. no. 44) and Carlo Magini (Exh. nos. 45 and 46) conclude the representation of this late phase. Both were painters who were content to pursue careers in the provinces. Magini worked in Fano in the Marches, and seems never to have left his native town. His career extended into the nineteenth century, and his highly personal style of still life is here proposed as an amalgam of the fashion for *trompe l'oeil* which arose in Florence earlier in the eighteenth century (under the influence of Cristoforo Munari) and of the sharply objective style of observation which was current in European painting at the turn of the nineteenth century immediately before the invention of photography. His predecessor by a full half-century, Arcangelo Resani pertains more clearly to the seventeenth-century traditions of Italian still life, although he lived until 1742. Resani was trained in Rome, and made his critical reputation in Bologna before transferring to Ravenna and other quiet towns of Romagna. As is discussed in the entry for the artist's masterpiece, here exhibited, Resani's still life paintings evince a poignancy and sense of spiritual withdrawal rarely encountered in the works of his Italian contemporaries.
In sum, this exhibition looks out over only the pinnacles in the whole range of Italian still life painting during the time of the Old Masters. The distinctions between the regional schools of Italy — the Roman style as opposed to the Neapolitan, for instance — remained significant even while the activity of foreign artists, especially Flemings, eventually gave rise to the formulation of a sort of *lingua franca*, a universally understood conception of still life decoration. The endless possibilities of subject matter and

rmat embraced by the Italian school constituted a situation quite
1like that found elsewhere in Europe. With the exception of the
2hesive character of Neapolitan still life painting during the
3venteenth century, the Italian tradition derived its vitality
3ostly from the achievements of individual masters. Roberto
3onghi's meditations on Caravaggio and Baschenis are based on
3is observation, strictly applied. A more expansive vision of the
3lues of Italian still life painting lay behind the present selection,
3hich has been made in the hope that the viewer will be inspired
3 further inquiry.

Following the example of historians of Netherlandish painting, it has lately
3en proposed by Barry Wind (1977) that Vincenzo Campi's paintings of
3ulterers, etc., at Kirchheim (cfr. Exh. nos. 1 and 2) are not scenes of pure
3enre", or daily life, rather they are invested with allegorical significances. This
3ew is shared by the present writer, who finds corroboration of it in another
3ombard painting of Fruit Vendors, this dated 1601, in the Wadsworth Atheneum,
3artford (R.P. 3). The style of this anonymous picture suggests the authorship of
3. B. Crespi, Il Cerano, the leading artist in Milan at this time. The odd gesture of
3e man who touches his windpipe can be explained by the flute in his hand and the
3eacock feather in his cap. The peacock was an attribute of the Roman goddess
3no, who governed the element of Air. The buxom woman who is washing lettuce
3ould seem in this context to personify the element of Water, which quantity is
3plied elsewhere in the painting in the onions, melons, lemons. It seems likely
3at this artist, perhaps Cerano, would have painted a pendant with allegories of
3rth and Fire, a picture at present untraced.

C. Sterling, 2nd rev. ed. 1981, pp. 25-33.

I. Bergström, 1956, p. 28 and p. 298 note 78.

Ibid., pp. 292-293. S. Segal, 1982, pp. 3-11.

Cf. I. Bergström, 1956, pp. 13-14, and S. Segal, 1982, p. 13.

The reader is referred to the invaluable text by I. Bergström, cited above, for
3ustrations and a detailed account of the most important developments in early
3etherlandish still life painting.

E. Gombrich, 1978, pp. 95-105. Similarly, I. Bergström, 1970, pp. 13-15, has
3inted out the Florentine sources of a series of frescoes of antique vases and
3wers painted by Juan de Borgoña in the Cathedral of Toledo, 1509-11.

This translation is adapted from E. Gombrich, 1978, p. 102.

A. Venturi, cited in *Ibid.*, p. 169 note 10.

3) In addition to Giovanni da Udine, Vasari especially praises the naturalism of
3e festoons and flowers painted by Camillo Mantovani (1568) in the Palazzo
3rimaldi, Venice, and the Palazzo Imperiale, Pesaro.

3) Vasari's phrase may deliberately reflect the original Greek term for still life,
3opography, the painting of insignificant objects. Cf. C. Sterling, 2nd rev. ed.
3981, p. 27.

3) R. Longhi, 1950, p. 35.

3) G. Bottari, 1768, VI, p. 247.

3) From the artist's statements at the Baglione libel suit; see W. Friedlaender,
3974, pp. 276-277. Caravaggio's phrase, *imitar bene le cose naturali* recalls
3asari's description of the subjects painted by Giovanni da Udine.

3) C. Sterling, 2nd rev. ed. 1981.

3) R. Causa, 1972, pp. 997-999; R. Causa, 1978.

3) C. Volpe in London, 1982, pp. 57-59.

3) A. Ottani Cavina, 1976, pp. 139-144.

3) R. P. Ciardi, 1968, pp. 104-105.

3) One of these specialists, Francesco Zucchi, was the subject of a separate
3iography by Baglione. Baglione describes, moreover, easel paintings by Zucchi:
3apricious personifications of the Four Seasons composed of appropriate produce
3nd flowers.

3) M. Gregori, 1973, pp. 36-56.

3) The theoretical underpinnings of classical style precluded the practice by
3omenichino, for instance, and other classicizing painters of the lowly genre of
3ill life. It is interesting that both Domenichino and Poussin were willing to
3ontribute figural compositions to the central portions of floral garlands painted by
3aniel Seghers during the Fleming's Roman sojourn, 1625-27.

23) R. Causa, 1961, pp. 344-353; *idem*, 1972, pp. 1003-1004, pp. 1036-1037
notes 23-26.

24) R. Causa, 1972, pp. 1004-1008. See also London, 1982, pp. 194-195; this
last reference arrived too late to be cited in the entries of the present catalogue.

25) See London, 1982, pp. 219-221, for a survey of our knowledge of G. B.
Recco, based mainly on the researches of R. Causa. A *Kitchen Interior* (ex-Astarita
Coll., Naples), monogrammed *G.B.R.*, has been ascribed to the artist by the same
scholar; if an early work, as Causa has proposed, then G. B. Recco would precede
Giovanni Domenico Valentino, a Roman painter of mid-century (R.P. 51 and 52),
as the proponent of a Dutch-influenced style of interior, i.e. a room filled with a
picturesque jumble of household items.

26) Luca Giordano played the major role in the organization of an exhibition of
fourteen large still life paintings in conjunction with the annual feast of *Corpus
Domini*, according to B. De Dominici, 1741, III, pp. 294, 296, 298, 442, 562. De
Dominici does not mention the year of this special observance of *Corpus Domini*,
but he identifies the Marchese del Carpio, who was Viceroy of Naples 1683-87, as
the patron of the event. It seems that Giordano was authorized to commission
canvases, 18 palmi in breadth, from the leading masters of still life in Naples and to
complete these compositions with the addition of figures by his own hand. De
Dominici informs us that these fourteen paintings also included some animal
subjects with figures by Giordano and that the following artists were invited to
participate: Giovan Battista Ruoppolo (four paintings of fruits, fish, and game);
Giuseppe Recco (two paintings of fish and sweetmeats); Abraham Brueghel
(fruits); and Francesco della Quosta (crustaceans and vegetables). None of these
paintings has ever been identified. Three likely candidates for the *Corpus Domini*
series were published (without comment) by U. Prota-Giurleo, 1953, pp. 80, 112,
144, as two still lifes and a *Flock of Sheep* by Luca Giordano, Zacchia-Rondinini
collection, Bologna. The latter picture (253x370 cm.) was subsequently acquired
by the Pinacoteca Nazionale and is dated to 1682-83 by A. Emiliani (1967), figs.
279, 280). Coincidentally, Prota-Giurleo (p. 61) published a reference to the sale
to a pair of Venetian merchants of eight large paintings by Luca Giordano for the
princely sum of 2400 ducats. Each of the eight canvases measured 10x14 palmi:
"Two [paintings] of fish with figures, two of herds with figures, two of grapes with
figures, and the other two of fruits and flowers with figures. All of the figures with
their accompaniment are from the hand of Luca Giordano". These descriptions
and the date of this transaction, April 1, 1684, support the conclusion that De
Dominici's account of the *Corpus Domini* exhibition of Neapolitan still life
paintings is substantially accurate.

Anonymous Lombard, ca. 1600   Exh. nos. 3, 4
Evaristo Baschenis   Exh. nos. 22, 23, 24, 25
Andrea Belvedere   Exh. nos. 40, 41
Bartolomeo del Bimbo   Exh. no. 38
Felice Boselli   Exh. no. 36
Abraham Brueghel   Exh. no. 34
Vincenzo Campi   Exh. nos. 1, 2
Michelangelo Merisi da Caravaggio, Anonymous Follower   Exh. nos. 8, 9, 10
Jacopo Chimenti da Empoli   Exh. no. 18
Pier Francesco Cittadini   Exh. no. 26
Luca Forte   Exh. nos. 14, 15, 16, 17
Fede Galizia   Exh. no. 5
Giovanna Garzoni   Exh. nos. 19, 20, 21
Giovanni da Udine, Follower of   Exh. no. 7
Carlo Magini   Exh. nos. 45, 46
Cristoforo Munari   Exh. no. 37
Giacomo Nani   Exh. no. 42
Panfilo Nuvolone   Exh. no. 6
'The Pensionante del Saraceni'   Exh. no. 11
Paolo Porpora   Exh. nos. 27, 28
Giuseppe Recco   Exh. nos. 31, 32, 33
Arcangelo Resani   Exh. no. 44
Giovan Battista Ruoppolo   Exh. nos. 29, 30
Tommaso Salini   Exh. nos. 12, 13
Giovanni Paolo Spadino   Exh. no. 39
Nicola Van Houbraken   Exh. no. 43
Antonio Maria Vassallo   Exh. no. 35

Catalogue

Catalogue

Vincenzo Campi
Cremona ca. 1530/35 - 1591 Cremona

Vincenzo Campi was the youngest of three artist sons of Galeazzo Campi, a painter in Cremona in North Italy. The eldest brother, Giulio Campi, founded the studio in which Antonio and Vincenzo were trained; together with Bernardino Campi (of undetermined relation), they comprised an artistic dynasty that was dominant in Lombard painting during the latter half of the sixteenth century. Vincenzo's date of birth is not known; however in 1566 Vasari already describes him as a "young man of great expectation". Vincenzo fulfilled his promise in more than one field of painting. As a painter of portraits and altarpieces and other devotional works he received prominent commissions in his native Cremona (in many churches, including frescoes in the Duomo, 1573), in Pavia (the Certosa, 1578; S. Francesco, before 1588), in Piacenza and Busseto in Emilia (ca. 1576-1581) and in Milan (where his presence is first documented in 1564 and lastly in 1588). Antonio Campi commented in his *Cremona fedelissima...*, 1585, that his younger brother had brought fame to himself and to Cremona, in which city his works were as prized as they were "in Milan and other places in Italy and also in Spain, where many have been sent."

Vincenzo's reputation today is based on his extensive and innovative production of genre paintings in which still life elements take precedence over the human figures. Campi's interest in such subjects, two of which are illustrated in this exhibition, was clearly inspired by the paintings of two prolific Netherlanders: Pieter Aertsen (1508/9-1575) (fig. 2) and his pupil, Joachim Beuckelaer (1530/35-1573/4). As S. Zamboni (1965) has pointed out, Vincenzo would have had ample occasion to see examples by these artists during his activity in Emilia in the latter 1570's: the Farnese collections in Parma included no fewer than seven paintings by Beuckelaer. Indeed, none of Vincenzo's paintings of still life *cum* genre are believed to date from before this period. Cremona was itself linked to the Netherlands by the bond of Hapsburg rule; moreover, the Affaitati family of Cremona, who were bankers to Charles V of Austria, were principally based in Antwerp.

A few independent still lifes (i.e. without figures) have been attributed to Vincenzo on the basis of stylistic comparison, but no signed or documented examples have as yet come to light.

1. The Fruit Vendor
Oil on canvas. 145x215 cm.
Provenance: From Cremona (1809); possibly painted for the *Foresteria* of S. Sigismondo, Cremona (cf. A. Perotti, 1932, p. 60
Selected References: F. Malaguzzi Valeri, 1908, p. 204; G. De Logu, 1931, p. 160, pl. 282; A. Venturi, 1933, IX(6), p. 898, fig. 553; Venice, Palazzo Ducale, 1951, no. 44, pl. 49; G. De Logu, 1962, p. 162, pl. 8; Naples, Palazzo Reale, 1964, no. 1, pl. 1a.; S. Zamboni, 1965, p. 134, fig. 49b; S. J. Freedberg, 1975, p. 589, fi 264; M. Rosci, 1977, p. 88; Münster and Baden-Baden, 1980, nc 147 (repr).
Milan, Pinacoteca di Brera (no. 333).

2. The Fish Vendors
Oil on canvas. 145x215 cm.
Provenance: From Cremona (1809); possibly painted for the *Foresteria* of S. Sigismondo, Cremona (cf. A. Perotti, 1932, p. 60
Selected References: F. Malaguzzi Valeri, 1908, p. 204; G. De Logu, 1931, fig. 285; Naples, Palazzo Reale, 1964, p. 23; M. Rosci, 1977, p. 88.
Milan, Pinacoteca di Brera (no. 334).

The *Fruit Vendor* and the *Fish Vendors* have been recognized as paired works by Campi since their removal to the Pinacoteca di Brera during the Napoleonic era (before 1908, they were attributed to Giulio Campi). In the present century, the *Fruit Vendor* has become the most admired painting in Vincenzo Campi's *oeuvre*, and has usually been discussed separately from its pendant. It has recently been discovered, however, that the *Fruit Vendor* and the *Fish Vendors* comprise half of a series of fou such depictions of peasant figures surrounded by commestibles: an additional two paintings of *Poulterers* (fig. 1) and a *Kitchen Scene* (fig. 2) were recently identified amongst the uncatalogued holdings of the Accademia di Brera. The four pictures are of identical size and were brought to Milan from Cremona together in 1809. They are here illustrated as a series for the first time, wit photographs made subsequently to their cleaning and restoratior

Fig. 1. Vincenzo Campi, Poulterers. *Accademia di Brera, Milan.*

in 1981 [1].

A comparable series of market scenes by Vincenzo Campi was executed on commission in 1580-81 for the Schloss Kirchheim residence of Hans Fugger, banker to the Hapsburg monarchy. They represent a *Fruit Vendor*, three different *Fish Vendors*, and *Poulterers* [2]. The last subject is an exact replica (or vice versa) of the Brera *Poulterers*. In addition, the grinning fish wife and her bawling baby in the Brera *Fish Vendors* appear again with other companions in two of the Kirchheim paintings of *Fish Vendors* (figs. 3 and 4).

The reconstitution of the Brera series raises the question of whether these four scenes of daily labor might have allegorical meanings in common. Artists and patrons in the late sixteenth century shared an erudite enthusiasm for allegorical representations of such natural phenomena as the Three Ages of Man, the Four Elements, and the Four Seasons. After 1575, and thus contemporaneous to Campi, Jacopo Da Ponte with his sons, Francesco and Leandro, made his Bassano studio into something like an assembly line for the serial depictions of such themes [3].

Because Vincenzo Campi did not include in the backgrounds of these market scenes diminutive depictions of Christian subjects, as Aertsen and Beuckelaer were wont to do, scholars have hitherto regarded the Brera *Fruit Vendor* and *Fish Vendors* as examples of pure genre, that is, scenes of everyday life. Indeed, it is true that Vincenzo's principal innovation in his paintings of this kind was his willingness to eschew Mannerist adornment in favor of an objective description of the sensuosity and substance of nature as our eyes perceive it. Campi's vision had profound import for the evolution of still life painting in Italy. Although motivated by Northern examples, Campi's style was based on the naturalistic roots of Lombard painting.

The exaggerated expressions and comical gestures of the actors in each of the Brera paintings — with the significant exception of the *Fruit Vendor* — were not derived from the precedents of Aertsen and Beuckelaer. In a recent iconographical study of Vincenzo's pictures at Kirchheim, Barry Wind has plausibly explained the artist's interest in fishmongers and poulterers as inspired by the ribald possibilities arising from the phallic connotations of those vendors' wares [4].

According to Wind, the Kirchheim series may be understood as a "sustained bawdy joke, similar in wit and piquant obscenity to the butcher shop paintings by Campi's Bolognese contemporaries, Passarotti and Annibale Carracci." [5] Wind points out as well that the beans that the fish vendors consume so lustily held similarly low anatomical associations for Cinquecento audiences.

Wind's analysis of the sexual imagery in Campi's series at Kirchheim applies clearly enough to the Brera *Fish Vendors* as well as to the newly recovered *Poulterers*. The coarse expressions amongst the helpers in the *Kitchen Scene* also allow for the possibility of latent sexual metaphors that await interpretation [6]. The *Fruit Vendor*, however, is evidently a case apart. The smile of the young maid is modest and her posture is demure. She carefully lifts a bunch of grapes by its stem.

As it happens, E. de Jongh has identified this very gesture — which occurs frequently in seventeenth century Dutch portraiture — as an emblem of virginity or marital chasteness [7]. De Jongh credited the invention of this emblem to the prolific Jacob Cats, who included in the 1618 edition of his emblem book,

Maechden-plicht, an illustration of grapes held aloft by their stem, accompanied by the motto, "Honor is fragile." [8] In the absence of corroborative evidence that this particular grape symbolism was known in Italy in the late sixteenth century, its application to Campi's picture must remain hypothetical. Still, the interpretation of the *Fruit Vendor* as an exemplar of chastity and a virtuous alternative [9] to the carnal activity (and *voluptas carnis* [10]) elsewhere in the Brera series is encouraged even by the contrast in the formal language between this picture and its three companions. Despite the eye-catching details of the abundant fruits, Campi composed the *Fruit Vendor* so that the contemplative maid would herself be the final focus of the viewer's attention, the apex of a pyramid of still life. By comparison, the convoluted, restless compositions of the *Fish Vendors, Poulterers*, and the *Kitchen Scene* can be appreciated as metaphors of their themes of promiscuity. If we are correct in discerning a moralistic distinction drawn between the virtuous maid and the other actors, then the Brera series could not be characterized as a joke: its intent would be moralizing although its means were humorous.

Finally, it is also possible that Campi's *Fruit Vendor* and *Fish Vendors* at the Pinacoteca di Brera and *Poulterers* and *Kitchen Scene* at the Accademia di Brera are mutually related as allegories of the four primary Elements: Earth, Water, Air, and Fire, respectively. Such an interpretation would constitute another level of meaning not exclusive to the moral lessons the series apparently presents. Besides the appropriateness of the still life elements as symbols of the fundamental Elements (fruits and vegetables of the earth, fish of the sea, birds of the air, and pies being readied for the oven), such details as the various landscape backgrounds support this theory. Perhaps it is not stretching a point to suggest that the element of Air provides an explanation for the puffed cheeks of the exasperated young man who grapples with an oversized fowl in the Brera *Poulterers*.

1) I am grateful to Carlo Bertelli for bringing the Accademia di Brera paintings to my attention. Prof. Bertelli very kindly arranged for me to view the four paintings by Campi during their restoration. It was interesting to note, in view of Campi's connections with Netherlandish artists, that the *Fish Vendors* was painted on a heavy linen of the kind that is described in Seicento Italian inventories as a "tela di fiandra."

2) B. Wind, 1977, figs. 1-5.

3) W. R. Rearick, 1968, p. 245.

4) B. Wind, 1977, p. 108f.

5) *Ibid.*, p. 108.

6) For instance, cheese, which is being grated in the center of the picture, was symbolic of copulation according to Wind, p. 112.

7) E. de Jongh, 1974, p. 166f. I am grateful to William W. Robinson and Frima Fox Hofrichter, both of whom mentioned this article to me.

8) *Ibid.*, fig. 2.

9) The peaches in the maid's lap add credence to this thesis, since they occur frequently in paintings as symbols of virtuous love.

10) J. Emmens, 1973, p. 95, in his study of the inverted compositions of Aertsen and Beuckelaer, suggests that the meats on display in the foreground have the negative connotation of *voluptas carnis*, or lust for the flesh (as opposed to faith in the Spirit). My thanks to Otto Naumann for bringing this article to my attention. For a contrary view, cf. K. Craig, 1982, p. 7.

3. Still Life with Apples and Pears
Oil on canvas. 43x54.5 cm.
Provenance: Private Collection, Florence.
Unpublished.
Campione d'Italia, Silvano Lodi Collection

4. Still Life with Birds and Fruit
Oil on canvas. 43x54.5 cm.
Provenance: Private Collection, Florence.
Unpublished.
Campione d'Italia, Silvano Lodi Collection.

The motif of a single raised salver, or *tazza*, filled with fruit is typically Lombard: all additional observations about the anonymous painter of this pair of still lifes must remain hypothetical pending the discovery of signed or otherwised documented works by this artist. The primary source for still life painting in Lombardy (besides North European examples) was identified by Roberto Longhi in the highly naturalistic vision of Alessandro Buonvicino, called Moretto (1498-1554), the late Renaissance master from Brescia [1]. Moretto was of course a painter of altarpieces, but his urge to create in paint a " nearly tangible duplicate... of unidealized reality " [2] was exercised as much on the inanimate attributes and symbols of the saints he portrayed as on their persons. Among the passages in Moretto that Longhi pointed out as prototypical for the development of independent still lifes, the basin of fruit (pl. 2) at the foot of the throne of the Madonna and Child in the alterpiece in S. Andrea, Bergamo (ca. 1540-45), has been cited repeatedly by scholars in this field. The comparison with Moretto reveals the extent to which our anonymous Lombard painter, working at least a half-century later , was enthralled with the decorative artifices of Mannerist style. The playful symmetry of the leaves and the fruits, not to mention the cherries that tumble out of the salver like life-lines tossed overboard, have been arranged to delight the viewer's sense of fantasy rather more than his recollections of nature. A similar rapprochement of observation and ornamentation can be observed in a passage of still life featured in a coeval painting (fig. 5) attributed to Simone Peterzano (documented 1573-1590), a leading exponent of the late Maniera in Milan and the master of Caravaggio.
The impressive projection of these two *tazzas* towards the viewer is an important contributor to their appeal. The massiveness of the individual elements (even the grapes are like miniature globes) is conveyed through the finely orchestrated use of deep shadows. In each painting, a focussed beam of light descends from upper left and organizes the picture between strong contrasts of light and shade. This system of shading apparently reveals our anonymous artist's knowledge of the chiaroscural developments in Caravaggio's paintings in Rome during the late 1590's. The exuberance with which the articles in this still life threaten to protrude beyond the picture margins on all sides might also indicate an early seventeenth-century date for these two pictures. An anonymous *Still Life with Peaches, Cherries, Pears and Beans* (Private Collection, Bergamo), which is — to judge from the photograph — by the same artist as the pair exhibited here, was attributed in 1971 to Pedro de Camprobín y Passano (1605 - post 1674), a Spanish still life specialist [3]. The painting in Bergamo was formerly attributed to the Lombard school. In fact, closely comparable treatments of leaves and stems can be found in abundance in paintings plausibly attributed to Camprobín [4]. However, there are no documented paintings by Camprobín in which the still life has been composed with such solitary, Italianate concentration as in this anonymous pair [5]. In any event, the juxtaposition of these two still lifes to the early Lombard paintings (cat. nos. 1, 2, 5, 6) and the Roman Caravaggesque paintings (cat. nos. 8, 9, 10, 11) in the present exhibition will undoubtedly suggest some answers to the many questions they pose.

1) R. Longhi, 1929, pp. 273-274.
2) S. J. Freedberg, 1975, p. 368.
3) I. Bergström, 1971, no. 43, pl. 43. The attribution to Camprobín was proposed by Pietro Lorenzelli.
4) Cf. Barcelona, Sala Parés, 1966, pls. XXXVI and XXXVII; Torres Martin, 1978, figure 6.
5) The opportunity for Camprobín to be closely influenced by a Lombard artist was readily provided by the political ties between Spain and Milan at that time.

Fig. 5. Simone Peterzano, Allegorical Figure. *Lodi Collection, Campione d'Italia.*

Fede Galizia was renowned in her own lifetime for her distinctions as a woman artist and an artistic prodigy. Before the age of twenty she had won an international reputation as a portraitist, and during her career she received several commissions for altarpieces in Milanese churches, including the high altarpiece of Santa Maria Maddalena in 1616.

The early sources do not mention Galizia's activity as a painter of still lifes, which silence may indicate the rarity of her still lifes or the lesser prestige of such subjects (or both). However, it is in this sphere of art that Galizia revealed her genius. Stefano Bottari (1963) has identified a corpus of about twenty still lifes by Fede Galizia: the attributions are based upon comparison with a painting formerly in the Anholt Collection, Amsterdam, signed on the reverse and dated 1602 [1]. The Amsterdam still life (present whereabouts unknown) establishes Galizia's precedence and influence as a specialist in still lifes since it is the earliest Italian still life to bear a specific date. Only a handful of still lifes, chief among them Caravaggio's *Basket of Fruit* of ca. 1595 in the Ambrosiana, Milan (pl. 1), are considered earlier in date.

Fede Galizia was the daughter of Nunzio Galizia, a miniaturist from Trento in North Italy, who worked in Milan. At the age of twelve her abilities were sufficiently in evidence to merit a brief notice in the *Idea del tempio della pittura* (1590) by G. P. Lomazzo: "she is devoting herself to the imitation of the most excellent [masters] of our art". Lomazzo's comment is so general that it may mean nothing at all, but we may justifiably suppose — given her training with her father — that Galizia's first efforts were miniatures after other artist's compositions. In a letter written from Milan in 1663 to Prince Leopoldo de' Medici in Florence, Galizia is cited as a "painter and miniaturist." [2] This last aspect of her *oeuvre* awaits rediscovery.

Among the supporters of Galizia's career was Paolo Morigia, a Jesuit scholar and historian. A portrait of Morigia by Galizia dated 1596 in the Ambrosiana depicts the learned cleric at work on a poem in praise of her talents. As Ann Sutherland Harris has noted, Galizia's style of portraiture hearkens back to the naturalistic traditions of the Renaissance in North Italy, specifically Moretto, G. B. Moroni and Lorenzo Lotto [3].

5. Still Life with Peaches in a Porcelain Bowl

Oil on panel. 30x41.5 cm.
References: Geneva, 1978, p. 128. no. 91; Münster and Baden-Baden, 1980, p. 178, no. 99.
Campione d'Italia, Silvano Lodi Collection.

All of the still lifes by Fede Galizia that have been identified to date subscribe to the compositional plan observable in this *Peaches in a Porcelain Bowl:* the principal element, which can otherwise be a basket or a raised dish, is centered on a shallow stage; a few smaller fruits or nuts are usually placed to either side and nearer to the edge of the platform.

As practiced by Galizia, this plan — inexhaustible in its simplicity — became characteristic of the Lombard school as a whole. The intimate scale of her pictures and her preferred use of panel as a support seem to reflect North European influence, while her capacity to compose still lifes of such robust compactness is distinctively Italian. In terms of motifs, Galizia had a Netherlandish counterpart in Ambrosius Bosschaert the Elder (born Antwerp, 1573) although no works of his are identifiable earlier than 1607 [4].

In her native Milan, Galizia's still lifes found an immediate forerunner in a masterly *Still Life with Peaches on a Plate* on panel by Ambrogio Figino (Lorenzelli Collection, Bergamo) (fig. 6). Figino's still life was apparently painted for a Milanese collection; its execution has been estimated to ca. 1595 on the basis of an encomiastic madrigal inscribed on its reverse [5]. The peaches in Figino's still life (his only known example) are notably idealized in comparison to Galizia's. Both artists are seeking to demonstrate perfection, only their definitions differ: Galizia's still life pertains to the palpable world of the seventeenth century.

Christian Klemm has recently commented that the portentious quality of light in this *Peaches in a Porcelain Bowl* must indicate the presence of a level of symbolic meaning [6]. The madrigal on the reverse of the Figino qualifies that still life as a sort of counter-*vanitas* in that Figino is celebrated as the victor over nature because his peaches are immune to decay. The same spirit

Fig. 6. Ambrogio Figino, Still Life with Peaches on a Plate. *Lorenzelli Collection.*

seems to inform Galizia's peaches, as we have said, but not perhaps the plums beside the bowl. It is possible to see three different stages of development amongst the fruits in this still life: the sprig of unripened plums, the peaches at the peak of perfection, and the pair of plums to the right that are slightly over-ripe. Transition denotes ephemerality, the essence of *vanitas*.

1) First published by C. Benedict, 1938, p. 305, fig. 14. See also S. Bottari, 1965, fig. 6.

2) F. Baldinucci, 1975, VI (appendix), p. 99.

3) A. S. Harris and L. Nochlin, 1979, p. 116.

4) I. Bergström, 1956, p. 56. Cf. fig. 44.

5) R. P. Ciardi, 1968, pp. 104-105. The panel was first published by R. Longhi, 1967, pp. 18f, who discovered its Milanese provenance and proposed to date the painting to the first years of the seventeenth century.

6) Münster and Baden-Baden, 1980, p. 178.

he critical reputation of Panfilo Nuvolone has especially
enefited from the new-found appreciation for Italian still life
aintings during the past half-century. A native of Cremona in
Jorth Italy, Nuvolone was first a beloved but undistinguished
upil of G. B. Trotti, called Il Malosso (1555-1619). By 1610
anfilo had transferred to Milan where he drew particular
ifluence from the stolid style of Camillo Procaccini (ca.
555-1629), another master for whom the seventeenth century
ame too soon [1]. [It is worth noting that Carlo Antonio Procaccini,
ne brother of Camillo, was an esteemed specialist in still lifes,
one of which have yet been identified.]
Juvolone executed numerous public commissions in Milan
icluding frescoes in the Sansoni chapel, Sant'Angelo (1610), in
. Domenico e Lazzaro (1618), an altarpiece in the church of the
Capuchins (1620), and decorations in a chamber of the Palazzo
Jucale (1626). He is last documented in 1631. Lanzi (1789)
haracterized Panfilo the painter as "diligent rather than
maginative."
rior to our own century, Nuvolone was best remembered as the
ather of two painters: Carlo Francesco (1608-1661), also called
Panfilo, and Giuseppe (1619-1703). In the aftermath of the
lisastrous plague of 1630/31, Carlo Francesco and Giuseppe
Juvolone were successively the leaders of the Milanese school of
ainting for the balance of the seventeenth century.
he reappearance in private collections of two signed and dated
till lifes (1617 and 1620) by Panfilo, however, has placed his
ritical reputation on a par with his sons' for the first time. After
'ede Galizia, Panfilo Nuvolone is considered the most important
naster of still life painting in Lombardy during the first third of
he century. Due to the popularity of the carefully balanced mode
f composition fostered by Galizia and Nuvolone, it has been
lifficult to make secure additions to his *oeuvre* from the
onsiderable number of anonymous candidates. Nuvolone's
fforts at still life were apparently not an isolated aspect of his
areer: an inventory completed in 1635 of the collection of the
Juke of Savoy in Turin describes three still lifes attributed to
Juvolone [2]. In the 1655 inventory of the vast collection of the
Marqués de Leganés in Madrid, Panfilo Nuvolone is credited with
" a painting of peaches and grapes with a salver " on panel [3].

6. Still Life with Peaches on a *Tazza*
Oil on panel. 50.5x48.5 cm.
Unpublished.
Campione d'Italia, Silvano Lodi Collection.

The few still lifes signed or plausibly attributed to Panfilo
Nuvolone reveal him a faithful adherent to models invented by
Fede Galizia, in particular to Galizia's still lifes of advanced date
in which the brushwork is freer and the sense of atmosphere more
apparent. This point is borne out by the comparison of Nuvolone's
Still Life dated 1620 in the Dubini Collection, Milan (fig. 7), with
the *Still Life with Pears* in the Lorenzelli Collection, Bergamo (fig.
8), which is believed to be a relatively late work by Galizia [4].
Similarly, the *Still Life with Peaches on a Tazza* attributed to
Nuvolone in this exhibition is painted with a confident touch; it is

Fig. 7. *Panfilo Nuvolone,* Still Life. *Dubini Collection, Milan.*
Fig. 8. *Fede Galizia,* Still Life with Pears. *Lorenzelli Collection, Bergamo.*

the artist's sensitivity to highlights — a Lombard trait — that elicits the impression of meticulous detail.

Roberto Longhi commented with regard to Fede Galizia and Panfilo Nuvolone that they presumably knew Caravaggio's *Basket of Fruit* in the Ambrosiana (pl. 1), but they cannot be said to have *seen* it [5]. Even more than Galizia, Nuvolone remained enamoured of the idealizations set out at the end of the sixteenth century by Ambrogio Figino (cf. fig. 6) and oblivious to the naturalism promulgated in Rome by another Lombard, Caravaggio. Nuvolone was open as well to Northern European suggestions towards a miniaturist conception of still life. Lombard collectors evidently had a sophisticated appreciation for the deliberate archaisms of his style; we might note the Cinquecentesque formality and the restricted sense of space with which this *Still Life with Peaches* is presented. As it happens, this nostalgia for the Renaissance was itself a major current in the Baroque Age that Nuvolone entered so reluctantly.

1) See N. W. Neilson, 1969, pp. 219-220 for some clarifications of Panfilo's chronology as usually stated.

2) See A. Vesme, 1897, p. 53, no. 469; also M. Rosci, 1977, p. 91 and p. 165 note 26.

3) J. Lopez Navio, 1962, p. 315, no. 1115: "una pintura de melocotones y ubas con una salba, de panfilo nuvolone, en tabla, de alto 1/2 bara menos dos dedos, y de ancho 3 b." This description corresponds to the still life in the Dubini collection, Milan (fig. 7).

4) S. Bottari, 1963, pp. 314-315. See also Naples, Palazzo Reale, 1964, no. 20.

5) Cited by M. Rosci, 1977, p. 91.

It is by no means established that Giovanni da Udine (Udine 1487-1561(?) Rome) painted any independent still life subjects. However as the leading assistant in the Roman workshop of Raphael with responsibility for ornamental motifs and stucco decorations *all'antica*, Giovanni is considered the Renaissance precursor of later specialists in still life. His contemporary biographer, Giorgio Vasari, praises in the highest terms Giovanni's gift for the painting of "every natural object" (*tutte le cose naturali*).

In 1952 Charles Sterling published a *Vase of Flowers with a Lizard* (Private Collection) inscribed *G D Udine/In Casa Spilimbergo/A°. 1538.* The severe, symmetrical composition of this still life was clearly inspired by sixteenth-century style. Sterling also made mention of a nineteenth-century archival reference to a still life signed and dated *G. d. Udine A. 1555* in a Neapolitan private collection. Giovanni da Udine's brief

recognition as a still life specialist on the basis of these two works has been suspended for the present by the convincing demonstration by Raffaello Causa in 1961 that both of these still lifes (he was able to publish a photograph of the second) can be dated by considerations of style to the seventeenth century [1]. In Causa's opinion, both of the paintings in question are pastiches probably by a Neapolitan artist. In the latest edition of his *Still Life Painting* (1982) Sterling remains inclined to view these two still lifes as copies at least of lost prototypes by Giovanni da Udine [2]. An outline of the long career of Giovanni da Udine might still therefore be in order. He was trained 1502-1506 in his native Udine in Northern Italy in the workshop of Giovanni Martino da Udine. Vasari informs us that Giovanni also studied briefly with Giorgione in Venice before being sent to complete his education in Rome with Raphael. According to the same source, Giovanni was inspired by a Fleming in the Raphael shop, also named Giovanni, towards the painting of animals and still life motifs. About 1514, Raphael entrusted Giovanni da Udine with the painting of the musical instruments in his *St. Cecilia* altarpiece (now Pinacoteca Nazionale, Bologna). Together Raphael and Giovanni explored the ancient Roman ruins and marvelled at the painted and plastered wall decorations, called "grotesques" after the subterranean locations of the ruins. Early in 1516 Giovanni was employed in the Vatican apartments of Cardinal Bibbiena to decorate the walls *alla grottesca*. In 1517-18, Giulio Romano, Giovanni Francesco Penni and Giovanni da Udine painted frescoes after Raphael's design in the Loggia of Psyche in the Farnesina villa. Giovanni da Udine's assignment in this fresco project was to paint the lush festoons of leaves and fruits that transform the loggia vault into the illusion of an arbour. The most complete exercise of Giovanni's re-creation of antique grotesque style is to be found in the Vatican *Logge*, 1518-19, again an undertaking of the Raphael shop, including Giulio Romano, Giovanni Francesco Penni, Perino del Vaga and Polidoro da Caravaggio. At this time, Giovanni added stucco decorations for which he had rediscovered through trial and error the antique formula.

After Raphael's death in 1520, Giovanni continued to work at prominent sites in Rome until the early 1530's, most notably with Perino in the Sala dei Pontefici (1521) in the Vatican. His paintings in the sacristy of S. Lorenzo, Florence, of ca. 1532-33 are lost. By 1535, the date of his marriage, Giovanni had returned to Udine. He is recorded at work in the Palazzo Grimani, Venice, ca. 1539-41. An ornamental frieze by him in the palace at Spilimbergo is dated 1555. In 1560 or thereabouts Giovanni was called to Rome to work on the west wing of the Vatican *Logge*, his last known commission.

Fig. 9. *After Polidoro da Caravaggio,* Monumental Vase. *Engraving by Cherubino Alberti, British Museum, London.*

POLYDORVS DE CARAVGIO·I

ROMÆ

7. Still Life with Flowers in a Sculpted Vase
Oil on canvas. 55x40 cm.
Unpublished.
Campione d'Italia, Silvano Lodi Collection.

This *Still Life with Flowers in a Sculpted Vase* is a fine example of the type of floral still life that has come to be associated with the name of Giovanni da Udine although at present none of these works, including the two such paintings that bear " signatures " by Giovanni (discussed above) have been demonstrated to date from the sixteenth century, let alone from the artist's lifetime [3]. All of the still lifes are, however, composed in accordance with Italian precepts of balance, absolute clarity, and antiquarianism that render them archaic in style in comparison to other still lifes at the turn of the seventeenth century. Without the discovery of additional and datable examples of these still lifes, it cannot be resolved whether some at least of these paintings (they are by

Fig. 10. After Polidoro da Caravaggio, Monumental Vase. *Engraving by Cherubino Alberti, Rijksmuseum, Amsterdam.*

different hands) are *retardataire*, as Charles Sterling maintains, which would imply the existence of prototypes now lost, or whether they were painted to satisfy the taste for neo-Cinquecentesque evocations on seventeenth-century terms, as Raffaello Causa proposes. In either event, it is clear that the anonymous author of this *Still Life with Flowers in a Sculpted Vase* was inspired as well by the early (and presumably contemporary) floral still lifes painted and drawn after the 1590's by North European artists such as Georg Hoefnagel (who worked in Italy), Georg Flegel and Jacques de Gheyn II. The delicacy of the handling, the relatively large scale of the flowers to the vase, and the preciosity of the golden vase itself are Northern in character. Konrad Oberhuber has pointed out that the design of this vase in antique style, including its frieze of figures, derive from engravings after frescoes painted ca. 1527 by Polidoro da Caravaggio on the facade (no longer visible) of the Palazzo Milesi Rome [4]. Polidoro's frescoes *en grisaille* were held paradigmatic of classical style by generations of artists in Rome. In the spaces between the windows of the Palazzo Milesi, Polidoro painted a series of monumental stone vases (without flowers) infused with his own rather fantastic interpretations of ancient art. These vases were engraved first in 1582 by Cherubino Alberti in a suite of prints entitled *vasi polidoreschi*. The anonymous painter of this *Still Life with Flowers in a Sculpted Vase* combined the vase and its figural group — representing a sacrifice ritual — from two different vases in Alberti's series (cf. figs. 9 and 10). We can be certain that our anonymous artist borrowed these motifs from engravings as opposed to the original frescoes (or other drawings after them) because the *Still Life* incorporates also the plinth upon which Alberti set his *vasi*. Because the vase and frieze in the *Still Life* are in reverse direction from Alberti's prints, it is possible that the painter was working from the copies etched in reverse after Alberti's *vasi polidoreschi* by Egidius Sadeler (published in Prague, 1605) or by an anonymous Frenchman (published in Paris, chez le Blond, undated); these copies are thus in the same directions as Polidoro's originals.
Oberhuber suggests an attribution of the *Still Life with Flowers in a Sculpted Vase* to a North Italian artist, possibly a Bolognese [5].

1) R. Causa, 1961, pp. 344-353; cf. fig. 152a, " Anonymous Neapolitan, XVII century", dated, however, 1553.
2) C. Sterling, 1981, p. 57, pl. 12. See also Naples, 1964, no. 3.
3) The attribution by F. Bologna, 1968, to Giovanni da Udine of a *Vase of Flowers* (Lorenzelli Collection, Bergamo) was refuted by F. Zeri's observation that the vase displayed the coat of arms of Cardinal Fausto Poli, who was raised to the purple in 1623 by Urban VIII. See R. Causa, 1972, p. 1037 note 28. Causa, 1972, p. 1003, attributes the Lorenzelli Collection *Vase* to Giacomo Recco.
4) In a letter, May 14, 1981.
5) In conversation, May 20, 1981.

or a discussion of Caravaggio's role in the development of Italian ll life paintings see the Introduction.

nly one independent still life by Michelangelo Merisi da aravaggio is known: the *Basket of Fruit* in the Pinacoteca mbrosiana, Milan (pl. 1). The *Basket of Fruit* was included in the ollection of paintings donated by Cardinal Federico Borromeo to e Ambrosiana in 1607; thanks to this early documentation, the inting is among the most secure attributions in Caravaggio's uvre as well as, of course, one of the central images of European t. On the basis of style, the *Basket of Fruit* has always been cognized as an early work from Caravaggio's first years in Rome the 1590's. Passages of still life are prominent in his paintings of gures from this period (cf. figs. 11, 12 and 13), and several storians have addressed themselves to the possible symbolic eanings of the fruits and flowers he depicted [1]. The *Basket of uit* is usually dated to 1596 (following a suggestion by Longhi) association with a letter written in that year to Cardinal ederico Borromeo by Cardinal Francesco Maria del Monte, aravaggio's first influential patron, in which del Monte refers to a rthcoming gift of some paintings [2].

he question of whether or not Caravaggio painted any other

independent still lifes remains problematic. If he did, they would presumably also date from the relatively uncharted years of his early career, given that the seventeenth-century sources for Caravaggio's life and career are mostly silent concerning pure still lifes from his hand. His two contemporary biographers, Giulio Mancini (1619/20) and Giovanni Baglione (1642) do not mention his activity in this new field of art, although Baglione praises at length the naturalness of the glass carafe with flowers painted by Caravaggio in the foreground of his *Luteplayer* (Hermitage, Leningrad).

On the other hand, Giovan Pietro Bellori (1672) credits Caravaggio with fostering through his own success the excellent and highly appreciated school of flower painting in Rome during Bellori's time. According to Bellori, Caravaggio was employed by Giuseppe Cesari, Il Cavalier d'Arpino, specifically as a painter of flowers and fruits. However, the only example cited by Bellori is in fact a repetition of Baglione's description of the vase of flowers depicted in the *Luteplayer*, as Walter Friedländer has pointed out [3]. Bellori's supposition in favor of Caravaggio as a still life painter finds implicit confirmation in a statement attributed to the artist by his patron Vincenzo Giustiniani: "Caravaggio said that it cost him as much effort to make a good painting of flowers as of figures." [4] If Caravaggio did paint other still lifes the memory of their authorship was not retained for long: attributions to Caravaggio for still lifes mentioned in seventeenth-century inventories are almost non-existent [5].

The outline of Caravaggio's biography, with emphasis on his early career, is as follows. The artist was born in 1571 in Caravaggio in

g. 11. Michelangelo da Caravaggio, Boy with Fruit (Bacchino Malato). *Galleria orghese, Rome.*

Fig. 12. Michelangelo da Caravaggio, Boy with a Basket of Fruit. *Galleria Borghese, Rome.*

Fig. 13. Michelangelo da Caravaggio, Bacchus. *Galleria degli Uffizi, Florence.*

Lombardy, the son of Fermo Merisi, who seems to have been located in Milan in the service of the marchese of Caravaggio. The family returned to Caravaggio after the death of Fermo Merisi in 1578. In 1584, Michelangelo Merisi was apprenticed in Milan for four years to the painter Simone Peterzano (cf. fig. 5); he was again resident in Caravaggio from 1589-1592. Probably at the end of 1592, the unproven and impoverished young artist made his way to Rome. No paintings from his student years in Milan and Caravaggio are known.

According to Mancini, Caravaggio's first employment was as factotum to one Pandolfo Pucci da Recanati, holder of a benefice from St. Peter's, who fed the artist nothing but salad, so that in later years Caravaggio referred to this first patron as "monsignor Insalata". For Pucci, Caravaggio painted several copies of devotional pictures for sale in Recanati (in the Marches). Mancini also writes that Caravaggio painted his earliest identifiable genre paintings while in the employ of Pandolfi Pucci: *A Boy Peeling an Apple* (recorded by several copies) and *A Boy Bitten by a Lizard* (Fondazione Longhi, Florence). At this time, Caravaggio fell gravely ill and was taken to the Ospedale della Consolazione, where during his convalescence, he painted many paintings for the hospital prior who took them either to Sicily or Seville (according to variant manuscripts of Mancini).

Baglione does not mention Pandolfo Pucci, but places the artist instead in an initial stay with an unnamed Sicilian painter of meager talent. Baglione believed that Caravaggio then entered the studio of Cavalier Giuseppe Cesari d'Arpino for several months. The same writer informs us that Caravaggio painted his *Boy with Fruit* (called the *Bacchino Malato*; Galleria Borghese, Rome) and the *Boy Bitten by a Lizard* during his stay with d'Arpino. His talent was recognized finally by Cardinal del Monte, who took the artist into his house ca. 1596/97 and rescued him from poverty. Mancini does not discuss in specific terms Cardinal del Monte's patronage of Caravaggio and it is from Baglione and from archival references (such as the 1627 inventory of the del Monte collection) that we learn that del Monte commissioned the genre subjects of Caravaggio's first maturity: the *Concert of Youths* (Metropolitan Museum of Art, New York); the *Luteplayer*; the *Cardsharps* (ex-Sciarra Collection, Rome); as well as the Ambrosiana *Basket of Fruit*, among other pictures.

G. P. Bellori begins his account of Caravaggio's career with references to his apprenticeship in Milan, as had earlier writers. Bellori further suggests that Caravaggio's first works in Lombardy were portraits, and that Caravaggio left Milan after an altercation coming to Rome by way of Venice. Caravaggio's unhappy employment as a painter of flowers and fruits for Cavalier d'Arpino is the only Roman occupation mentioned by Bellori prior to his adoption by Cardinal del Monte.

At the turn of the seventeenth century, Caravaggio was still resident in the house of del Monte but his circle of patronage was rapidly expanding to include marchese Vincenzo Giustinani and the noble houses of Pamphilj, Mattei, and Barberini. In July of 1599 Caravaggio received the commission formerly held by Cavalier d'Arpino to paint the two lateral paintings, *The Calling of St. Matthew* and *The Martyrdom of St. Matthew*, in the Contarelli Chapel, S. Luigi dei Francesi. Both paintings were in place in December 1600. On February 7, 1602, Caravaggio contracted to paint the altarpiece of the chapel, *St. Matthew and the Angel*, which was in place (second version) by September 1602. In the meantime, the artist had executed two lateral paintings, *The Crucifixion of St. Peter* and *The Conversion of St. Paul* for the Cerasi Chapel in S. Maria del Popolo. This commission was given in September 1600 and was completed by November 1601. These years of intense activity and accomplishment witnessed also the unfolding of a pattern of violent behavior by Caravaggio with increasingly frequent encounters with the law. (Less grave in consequence was the libel suit brought in August, 1603, by the painter Giovanni Baglione against Caravaggio, the presumed author of several indecent poems on the subject of Baglione.) During the winter of 1603-04 Caravaggio was briefly in Tolentino (in the Marches). His altarpiece of *The Entombment* (Pinacoteca Vaticana, Rome) was in place in the Cappella della Pietà in the Chiesa Nuova by September 6th, 1604. In April, October, November of 1604 and May, July, September and October of 1605, Caravaggio was either arrested or incarcerated on charges of assault or other disturbances of the peace. During the first months of 1606 the artist completed two altarpieces for major churches in Rome: *The Madonna di Loreto* (S. Agostino, Rome) and *The Madonna dei Palafrenieri* (for St. Peter's; now Galleria Borghese, Rome).

On May 20th, 1606 Caravaggio murdered his opponent in a dispute over a ball-game in the Campo Marzio and fled Rome. He received asylum in Zagarolo and other properties of Don Marzio Colonna in Lazio. In early October of the same year the fugitive

aravaggio had retreated to the more prudent distance of Naples
nd had already received lucrative commissions from several
ources. His monumental altarpiece of *The Seven Acts of Mercy* in
ne Pio Monte della Misericordia, Naples, was completed before
nuary 1607. Caravaggio received two payments in May of 1607
n account for an altarpiece in S. Domenico Maggiore, *The
agellation* (on deposit with the Museo di Capodimonte,
aples). During the summer (documented July) Caravaggio
isited Malta. He had evidently been in residence in Malta for at
·ast several months, when on the 13th July, 1608, he was received
ato the Order of St. John of Jerusalem, Rhodes and Malta as a
night of Obedience. In gratitude for this honor, Caravaggio
ainted his monumental *The Beheading of St. John the Baptist* for
ne Oratory of the Conventual Church of St. John, Valletta. By
)ctober, 1608, however, Caravaggio had been incarcerated for an
nknown offense and had fled from Malta to Sicily. In the space of
year, he stopped at Syracuse, Messina and Palermo, executing
ltarpieces in each city. When this work was finished he felt that it
·as no longer safe to remain in Sicily: he returned to Naples with
ne hope of receiving news from Rome of a pardon. During the
·inter of 1609/10 Caravaggio convalesced from a serious wound
·ceived in an attack in Naples in October. In July 1610
·aravaggio sailed from Naples to Port'Ercole (north of Rome). He
ontracted there a fever and died on the 18th July 1610.

8. Still Life with Flowers and Fruit
Oil on canvas. 105x184 cm.
Provenance: ? From Giuseppe Cesari, Il Cavalier d'Arpino,
Rome, 1607.
References: See P. Della Pergola, 1959, II, no. 287, for earlier
bibliography and attributions to Karel van Vogelaer or " Flemish
school ". F. Zeri, 1976, pp. 92-103, fig. 91 (as Caravaggio); C.
Strinati, 1979, pp. 62-65, pl. 10 (attributed to Caravaggio).
Rome, Galleria Borghese.

9. Still Life with Birds
Oil on canvas. 103.5x173 cm.
Provenance: Probably from Giuseppe Cesari, Il Cavalier
d'Arpino, Rome, 1607.
References: See P. Della Pergola, 1959, II, no. 248, for earlier
bibliography and attributions to " Flemish master " and Arcangelo
Resani. F. Zeri, 1976, pp. 92-103, fig. 92 (as Caravaggio); C.
Strinati, 1979, pp. 62-65, pl. 11 (" attributed to Caravaggio ").
Rome, Galleria Borghese.

The *Still Life with Flowers and Fruit* and the *Still Life with Birds*
exhibited together here were unknown in the literature on Italian
still life painting prior to their publication by Federico Zeri in a
provocative and brilliantly-argued article of 1976 [6]. Formerly
attributed to different Flemish hands, these two paintings from
the reserve collection of the Galleria Borghese became central
works in Zeri's proposed reconstruction of the young
Caravaggio's " lost " production as a painter of flowers and fruits
in the atelier of Cavalier d'Arpino, ca. 1593. As discussed above,
the documentary evidence relative to Caravaggio's possible
activity as a still life specialist is scant, but not negligible.
Zeri has reopened this inquiry with two important contributions.
First of all, he has compiled the photographs of a group of still lifes
which he has plausibly attributed to a single master. For Zeri, this
master must be Caravaggio, newly arrived in Rome. The paintings
presented by Zeri are closely interrelated, in fact, and they
conform to our conception (rough as it is) of the style of still life
painting in Rome at the turn of the seventeenth century. The
present exhibition will provide scholars — and the American
public — with the opportunity to confirm or deny Zeri's proposal
of common authorship for the two paintings from the Galleria
Borghese and for the *Still Life with Flowers and Fruit* lent by the
Wadsworth Atheneum in Hartford (see Exh. no. 10): these three
paintings are the core of this hypothetical *corpus*.
In the opinion of this writer, the Borghese still lifes are most likely
by the same hand, and the Hartford painting appears to be
another, slightly advanced work by this same artist of
controversial identity.
To support his thesis, Zeri has also re-examined some
documentation whose value for the study of still life painting in
Rome had previously been overlooked. Already in 1959, Paola
della Pergola has suggested in the catalogue of the Galleria
Borghese that the *Still Life with Birds* could be identified with a
reference in an inventory of the paintings that were confiscated by
papal authority in 1607 from the house of Cavalier d'Arpino (and
thereafter came into the possession of Cardinal Scipione
Borghese) [7]. Unfortunately for our purposes, this inventory gives
only brief descriptions of the paintings without indication of

8

artist. However, in the absence of an alternative in the Borghese collection, the association of the *Still Life with Birds* with the inventory reference (no. 38) to " A picture with various dead birds, unframed " is reasonable. Zeri proceeds from this likelihood of a d'Arpino provenance for the *Still Life with Birds* to propose the same for the *Still Life with Flowers and Fruit* on the basis of the very next item in the d'Arpino inventory (no. 39) : " Another picture with various fruits and flowers, unframed ". Moreover, Zeri would identify the Hartford *Still Life with Flowers and Fruit* (see Exh. no. 10, below) and one other painting in his compilation of attributions with the summary descriptions in this inventory. In favor of Zeri's point of view is the general consensus among scholars that two famous paintings by Caravaggio from the period ca. 1593-95, the *Boy with Fruit* (*Bacchino Malato*) and the *Boy with a Basket of Fruit*, entered the Galleria Borghese with the d'Arpino confiscation and can be identified with entries in the inventory of 1607.

Zeri's researches into the provenance of the Galleria Borghese and the Hartford still lifes (Exh. nos. 8-10) have established a putative *terminus ante quem* of 1607 for the execution of these three paintings — the earliest documented date for still lifes of the Roman school. As Zeri points out, Caravaggio is the only artist recorded in the sources as having painted naturalistic still lifes in the ambient of Cavalier d'Arpino. However, the inventory of paintings confiscated by Paul V from Cavalier d'Arpino totalled more than one-hundred paintings (mostly unframed) of every description, from landscapes to genre subjects to numerous still lifes: in sum, the stock-in-trade of a picture dealer (as Donald Posner first observed [8]) and most improbably the production of his atelier alone. Zeri rules out the possibility that the still lifes discussed by him were painted by a follower of Caravaggio on the grounds that Caravaggio would not yet have had followers in 1593 so soon after his arrival in Rome. However, the evidence does not allow us to date the Borghese still lifes *et cetera* more specifically than *ante* 1607, nor have we any indications as to when or whence Cavalier d'Arpino acquired these pictures. By 1607, of course, it is safe to assume that many still life painters in Rome were working under the influence of Caravaggio, although undoubtedly without being able to assimilate his naturalistic manifesto all at once. The majority of these artists remain unidentified, but among them must have been Tommaso Salini (see Exh. nos. 12 and 13) whose early still life style is as yet unknown to us. Salini was already active in 1603 (he was a hostile witness at Caravaggio's libel trial), and Baglione maintained that Salini was " the first to arrange and to paint flowers with their leaves in vases, with various unusual and capricious compositions. " [9]

The circumstantial evidence for the attribution of these still lifes to Caravaggio is therefore far from compelling. The direct comparison of these paintings to the still life elements in the paintings from the artist's standard *oeuvre*, such as the *Bacchino Malato* and *Boy with a Basket of Fruit* of ca. 1594, is likewise discouraging. Prof. Zeri does not confront the still lifes in his hypothetical *corpus* with undoubted examples by Caravaggio, except to observe: " In the *Flowers and Fruits* of the Galleria Borghese and in the two canvases of Hartford and ex-Mont collection, the description of the wicker basket is so similar to that depicted in the *Boy with a Basket of Fruit* in the Galleria Borghese

that they very nearly could be superimposed over one another. " [1] In point of fact, the differences between the baskets painted by th anonymous artist and by Caravaggio are glaring. The inability of the anonymous artist to convey the texture of straw as well as his insensitivity to the subtly varied shadows cast by the leaves leaning over the side of the basket eliminate him from consideration as the same master who " defeated nature " in his ostensibly coeval *Boy with a Basket of Fruit*. In a recent study, C. Strinati upheld Zeri's attribution of the two Galleria Borghese sti lifes to Caravaggio although he was constrained to explain the inept treatment of the wicker basket as a lapse that one could expect to find even in the work of a master like Caravaggio [11]. The hypothesis advanced by Zeri does not address the issue of antecedents for the style of the Galleria Borghese still lifes. Claudio Strinati sees them as reflective of the still life compositions in Vincenzo Campi's genre paintings (Exh. nos. 1 and 2) and of the natural historical attitudes practiced in Florenc by Jacopo Ligozzi in his still life/scientific illustrations in tempera on paper (pl. 3).

Neither Zeri nor Strinati comment on the unmistakeably Roman, as opposed to Lombard, character of the Galleria Borghese and Hartford still lifes. In Roman still lifes, such as these, the shadows serve to underscore the plastic, volumetric qualities of the objects without disturbing the integrity of their outlines. (Compare the Lombard paintings in this Exhibition, nos. 1-6). Moreover, the arrangement of the elements in the Galleria Borghese and Hartford still lifes does not conform to Cremonese (i.e. Lombard or Florentine practice, but is typical of the Roman late Maniera both in the positioning of prominent motifs to frame the composition on either side and in the multiple foci in the center o the picture. On the contrary, the still life elements in Caravaggio's *Bacchino Malato* and *Boy with a Basket of Fruit* (and in the copie of his lost *Boy Peeling Fruit* of ca. 1593) are conceived in terms of tone and are manifestly Lombard in inspiration with sources in th still life passages of Moretto da Brescia (as Longhi saw so well; cf the discussion in Exh. nos. 3 and 4). Even in the cradle, so to speak, the artist Caravaggio strove to achieve his genius for pictorial unity. He also found the means of the Venetian Renaissance conducive to his goal and thus used chiaroscuro — even in his early, " blond " paintings — and a predominant diagonal axis in his compositions to direct the viewer's response t the subject. The Galleria Borghese and Hartford still lifes bespeak the impression made on an as yet unidentified Roman artist by the precepts for which Caravaggio was known even in North Europe as early as 1603: " He holds that all works are nothing but bagatelles, child's work, or trifles, whatever their subject and by whomever painted, unless they are done and painted after life and that nothing could be better than to follow nature. " [12] The autho (or authors) of the Galleria Borghese and Hartford still lifes resolved as early as 1607 to paint without adornment the simples creations of nature with all their blemishes and to present them as directly as possible. These ideas were bold at the advent of the seventeenth century and they were crucial to the rise of the Baroque.

Zeri has remarked that the grapes, figs, squash and nuts depicted in the Galleria Borghese *Still Life with Flowers and Fruit* represen indiscriminately all four seasons of the year, an indication that the picture does not pertain to a Four Seasons cycle. On the other

hand, a level of allegorical significance is clearly present in the *Still Life with Birds* in the form of a venerable symbol of Western art, the owl. As if the watchman in this aviary graveyard, a single, living owl at center left fixes his stare on the viewer. The symbolic associations of the owl are myriad: in the present context, the owl's reputation as a killer of other birds, and therefore as a *memento mori* certainly seems appropriate. According to Heinrich Schwarz, the representation of the owl in the market and kitchen scenes painted by Pieter Aertsen — which were well-known in North Italy — was probably a disguised symbol for gluttony and lasciviousness [13].

1) See the sections on *Iconologia* in the catalogue entries compiled by M. Marini, 1974, cat. nos. 2, 4-8, 16, 19, for the bibliography prior to that date; cf. also H. Röttgen, 1974, pp. 173-196.

2) R. Longhi, ed. 1968, IV, p. 94. M. Marini, 1974, p. 361, quotes the letter in its entirety.

3) W. Friedlaender, 1974, p. 80 and pp. 142-143.

4) G. Bottari, 1768, VI, p. 247.

5) One exception is notable: a small painting of a carafe with flowers was attributed to Caravaggio in the 1627 inventory of the property of the deceased Cardinal F. M. del Monte and also in the subsequent sale of the del Monte collection on the 8th May 1628. See C. L. Frommel, 1971/72, p. 31 and M. Marini, 1974, cat. no. P-5 (p. 472). This untraced still life has frequently been associated with Bellori's description of a *caraffa di fiori* (See above and note 3).

6) F. Zeri, 1976, pp. 92-103.

7) P. della Pergola, 1959, no. 248 and p. 195. The inventory is published in A. De Rinaldis, 1936, III, no. 2, pp. 110f. R. Causa, 1972, pp. 998 and 1034 note 7, rightly pointed to this inventory as possible evidence of lost works by Caravaggio, but more likely an indication of the immediate impression made by Caravaggio in the d'Arpino ambient.

8) D. Posner, 1971, pp. 315-316.

9) G. Baglione, ed. 1649, p. 288. See Exh. no. 12 note 5, below, for early references to flower still lifes by Salini.

10) F. Zeri, 1976, p. 101.

11) C. Strinati, 1979, p. 64.

12) K. van Mander, *Het Schilder-Boeck*, 1603 [ed. 1604], Haarlem, quoted and translated in W. Friedlaender, 1974, pp. 259-260.

13) H. Schwarz and V. Plagemann, 1973, pp. 306-307. Owls are placed prominently in *Kitchen Scenes* by Aertsen in the National Museum, Stockholm, 1562 and Statens Museum for Konst, Copenhagen, 1572 (R. P. fig. 2).

10. Still Life with Flowers and Fruit

Oil on canvas. 71x96.5 cm.
Provenance: Acquisition, The Ella Gallup Sumner and Mary Catlin Sumner Collection fund, 1944.
References: *Art News*, May 1944 (repr. as. "Fede Galizia"); C. Sterling, 1952, p. 88 no. 66 (as anonymous copyist of Caravaggio 1615-20); C. Sterling, 1959, pl. 55 (Follower of Caravaggio); S. Bottari, 1963, p. 318 note 29 ('not by Fede Galizia'); Hartford, 1963, no. 9 (Follower of Caravaggio; ca. 1630); A. Moir, 1967, I, p. 27 note 19 (a northern European master; repr. fig. 24 as Fede Galizia); S. Ostrow, 1968, no. 6 (Italian Follower of Caravaggio, ca. 1630); R. Causa, 1972, pp. 1032-33 note 6 (as an anonymous Roman artist in the Caravaggesque ambient); C. Volpe, 1972 (1) p. 74 (a Caravaggesque master in the circle of G. B. Crescenzi); C. Volpe, 1972 (2), cat. no. 9; M. Gregori, 1973, p. 42f, fig. 24 ("Master of Hartford, before 1610"); F. Zeri, 1976, pp. 92-103 *passim* (Caravaggio); M. Rosci, 1977, pp. 95, 98, 166 note 67, 200 (Master of the Hartford Still Life); R. Causa, 1978, p. 41; C. Strinati, 1979, p. 62; C. Sterling, 2nd rev. ed. 1981, p. 17, pl. 55 (Follower of Caravaggio).

Hartford, Wadsworth Atheneum

Charles Sterling was the first to recognize the Roman and specifically Caravaggesque character of this *Still Life with Flowers and Fruit*, previously ascribed to Fede Galizia. During the past three decades the painting has been constantly under discussion by historians. The attributions proposed for this otherwise unpretentious picture have ranged parabolically, one might say, from Sterling's original hypothesis that it recorded a lost original by Caravaggio, to a consensus among scholars that its author was an early seventeenth-century Roman follower of the Lombard, and most recently, to Federico Zeri's suggestion that the "Master of Hartford" was Caravaggio himself.
A summary of Zeri's proposals appears in the entry for Exh. nos. 8 and 9. The crux of his hypothesis is his identification of the Hartford *Still Life with Flowers and Fruit* as a painting by the same artist as two still lifes in the Galleria Borghese (Exh. nos. 8 and 9) which seem to have been in the possession of Cavalier d'Arpino before 1607. The present exhibition marks the first occasion to compare these three paintings side-by-side and to test Zeri's observation of a single hand: for Zeri, the young Caravaggio, ca. 1593, working in the d'Arpino studio.
The attribution of the Galleria Borghese still lifes (and by implication, of the Hartford picture) to Caravaggio was repeated by C. Strinati in the catalogue of a 1979 exhibition in Rome, where the issue excited much debate. Charles Sterling (1981) has commented most recently that "This identification is to be considered very seriously, and its historical implications are far reaching." Raffaello Causa (1978) and Marco Rosci (1977) have rejected the possibility of Caravaggio's authorship of the Hartford still life. For reasons cited in the previous entry, the present writer agrees with earlier scholars that the painter in question should be considered an anonymous follower of Caravaggio, representative of the "first reaction by the [still life] specialists of the Roman ambient" (Causa, 1972) and active in Rome before the "beginning of the second decade" (Gregori, 1973, p. 43).
An important aspect of Zeri's contribution is the convincing *corpus* of other still lifes he has associated with the Hartford

Fig. 14. Anonymous Follower of Caravaggio, Still Life. *Formerly Mont Collection, New York.*

picture. In all, Zeri illustrates seven paintings besides the Hartford still life: all of these, except for the Galleria Borghese pictures, depict glass carafes and flowers that are closely comparable. According to Zeri, the Hartford still life would be the most advanced, i.e. latest in date, of the group, preceded by the Galleria Borghese pair. In addition to still lifes by the Hartford Master that were previously identified by Mina Gregori and Carlo Volpe, Zeri published a major example formerly with Frederick Mont in New York (fig. 14). The Mont canvas presents a veritable compendium of motifs in early Italian still lifes: the carafe, basket and bunch of wild strawberries are typically Roman; the *tazza* and the "Turkey Carpet" evoke Lombard still lifes.

One of the most impressive personalities amongst the expatriate artists in Rome during the early Seicento was the anonymous Caravaggesque painter known today as the "Pensionante del Saraceni." The hand of the Pensionante was first identified by Roberto Longhi in 1943 in several Caravaggesque paintings strongly influenced by Carlo Saraceni — hence the sobriquet coined by Longhi, which means "Saraceni's boarder". Longhi also noticed a "certain intonation, a certain French accent" in the Pensionante's works, to wit the *Fruit Vendor* in the Detroit Institute of Arts; the *Fishmonger*, Corsini Collection, Florence; the *Poultry Vendor*, Prado, Madrid; and *Job Mocked by His Wife*, the Vatican Museums. It is now generally agreed by scholars that the Pensionante must have been a Frenchman in Rome. Convincing additions to the *oeuvre* outlined by Longhi have included other versions of the Vatican *Job Mocked* and a bustlength *St. Jerome* [1]. Benedict Nicolson and Pierre Rosenberg have both observed that the intimate, almost diffident sensibility of the Pensionante, together with his Caravaggism, qualify him as a possible influence on Georges de la Tour [2].

Since 1954 and the subsequent acceptance of Fritz Baumgart's attribution of the *Still Life with Fruit and Carafe* in the National Gallery, Washington, to the Pensionante del Saraceni, the artist has been recognized as a pivotal figure in the development of Roman still life painting in the decade of 1610-1620, between the initial responses to Caravaggio's naturalistic innovations and the subsequent flowering of the Baroque.

11. Still Life with Fruit and Carafe
Oil on canvas. 51x72 cm.
Provenance: Fejer de Buck Collection, Rome; Contini Bonacossi, Florence; Samuel H. Kress Collection, New York.
Selected References: R. Longhi, 1928/29, p. 274 (as Caravaggio); R. Longhi, 1943, p. 23; B. Berenson, 1951, p. 9 (as Caravaggio); F. Baumgart, 1954, p. 201 note 28 (as "Pensionante del Saraceni"); C. Sterling, 1952, p. 53 (as follower of Caravaggio); A. Ottani Cavina, 1968, p. 68 note 48; R. Causa, 1972, p. 1032 note 6; F. R. Shapley, 1973, pp. 65-66, fig. 121; R. Spear, 1975, p. 138, fig. 34; B. Nicolson, 1979, p. 78; F. R. Shapley, 1979, I, pp. 112-114, II, pl. 77; P. Rosenberg, 1982, p. 299. A complete bibliography is given in F. R. Shapley, 1979, pp. 112-114, and additions are cited in P. Rosenberg, 1982, p. 299.
Washington D. C., National Gallery of Art.

The fame of this *Still Life with Fruit and Carafe* derives in part from the illustrious name it bore for many years — that of Caravaggio — but equally from its singular impressiveness [3]. Roberto Longhi never relinquished the attribution to Caravaggio that he had advanced in 1928/29, undoubtedly convinced (despite the mounting evidence) that no other artist of this moment could have depicted the simple elements of a meal with a clarity bordering on grandeur. Already in 1952, however, Charles Sterling had reassigned the *Still Life* to a "faithful pupil" of Caravaggio. Soon thereafter, Fritz Baumgart (1954) related the picture to the *corpus* of paintings assembled by Longhi himself under the heading of the anonymous "Pensionante del Saraceni". In the aftermath of the *Caravaggio and his Followers* exhibition in Cleveland in 1972, in which the Pensionante's *Fruit Vendor* (Detroit Institute of Art) was included, virtually every writer on the artist has seen the Pensionante's hand in the present *Still Life with Fruit and Carafe* on the basis of the comparison with the still life passages in the Detroit picture (fig. 15). All that remained to conclude the discussion was the actual juxtaposition of the two paintings next to one another: this ideal situation was among the benefits of the monumental exhibition, *France in the Golden Age, Seventeenth-Century French Paintings in American Collections*, organized this year (1982) by Pierre Rosenberg for the Louvre, the Metropolitan Museum of Art, and the Art Institute of Chicago [4]. Interestingly enough, only the basket of fruit in the *Fruit Vendor* displays identically the highly controlled technique observable throughout the Washington *Still Life*. The two varieties of melon shown on the table in front of the vendor were painted in a freer, more atmospheric manner, one that is actually more characteristic of the Pensionante's works so far as we know them. These broader passages are more sensuous in their appeal to the sense of touch, and seem to evince the Pensionante's awareness of Bolognese style. Finally however, in the context of the *France in the Golden Age* exhibition, the Frenchness of the Pensionante was confirmed by the ease with which his works were inserted amongst the French *Caravaggisti*. The same point should emerge, by contrast, from the present gathering of Italian still lifes. In a photograph, the Pensionante's *Still Life with Fruit and Carafe* appears to proffer fruits as imposing in their bulk as could be found in any Italian picture. At heart, however, the Pensionante was more concerned with the roundness of his forms than with

Fig. 15. Pensionante del Saraceni, Fruit Vendor. *Detroit Institute of Art.*

their massiveness, and thus proved himself a countryman of the artist who advised a colleague exactly three centuries later, "Treat nature in terms of the cylinder, the sphere, the cone..." [5] Pierre Rosenberg has remarked that if the Pensionante del Saraceni returned to France after his Roman activity, as his elusiveness in the Italian sources would indicate, his momentous conception of still life nevertheless made no impression on French specialists. On the other hand, this *Still Life with Fruit and Carafe* (and any others from his hand) were as a bridge between the first wave of Italian responses towards Caravaggio, which are marked by a diffuseness of composition (cf. Exh. nos. 8-10),and the realization of Baroque style which this *Still Life* anticipates through the irresistable rhythm of movement that unifies the foreground and background planes as the composition unfolds from left to right: melon, carafe, dish, melon and pear [6].

1) See the list of works in B. Nicolson, 1979, pp. 77-78. In addition, another version of the *Job Mocked* appeared recently on the auction market in New York (Sotheby Parke Bernet, 30 May 1979, lot 190, color pl.).
2) B. Nicolson and C. Wright, 1974, p. 33.
3) The picture seems to have been ascribed to Caravaggio even in the seventeenth century, to judge from an old label on its back (the authenticity of which has not been questioned, *contra* F. R. Shapley, 1979, p. 113 note 3).
4) See P. Rosenberg, 1982, pp. 298-299 for a valuable analysis of the Pensionante del Saraceni.
5) Paul Cezanne, in a letter to Emile Bernard of 15 April 1904. See the essay by T. Reff in W. Rubin, ed., 1977, p. 46.
6) R. Causa, 1972, p. 1032-33 note 6, aptly contrasted the movement in the Washington *Still Life* with the "monolithic and petrous" presence of the *Basket Fruit* in the Ambrosiana, Milan.

Tommaso Salini
Rome ca. 1575 - 1625 Rome

If not for the biography afforded him by his friend, Giovanni Baglione (1642), Tommaso Salini's career would be unknown to us except for a few stray references. Born in Rome of Florentine parents, Tommaso Salini, called "Mao", is first recorded as a witness against Caravaggio in the libel suit brought by Baglione in August 1603. From his testimony it can be deduced that he had been a painter for at least two years. Caravaggio claimed to have never seen a picture by him [1]. Salini's residence in the parish of S. Lorenzo in Lucina is documented in the years 1615, 1619, and 1623; in this last year he is described as *Cavaliere* [2]. Baglione reports that Salini was *Cavaliere dello Speron d'oro*. Notwithstanding his personal loyalties, Salini executed altarpieces in Caravaggesque style for several important Roman churches: S. Agnese in Piazza Navona; S. Lorenzo in Lucina; and two for S. Agostino. These works are now untraced with the exception of his altarpiece from the chapel of St. Nicholas of Tolentino, S. Agostino, which was removed to the church convent. In 1618 Salini donated a painting of *The Ecstasy of St. Francis* (SS. Luca e Martina) to the Accademia di S. Luca in gratitude for his admission in that year [3].

The name Tommaso Salini was introduced into the scholarship of Italian still life painting by Roberto Longhi in a famous article of 1950. On the basis of his readings of Baglione's *vite* Longhi identified Salini, together with Pietro Paolo Bonzi and G. B. Crescenzi, as the critical figures in the development of Roman still life painting in the aftermath of Caravaggio. Unfortunately, secure attributions of still lifes by this triad of painters are rare or non-existent (Crescenzi). Baglione wrote enthusiastically about Salini's paintings of "flowers and fruits and other natural things." He remarked, moreover, that Salini was "the first to arrange and to paint flowers with their leaves in vases, with various unusual and capricious compositions." [4]

References to still lifes, especially flower paintings, by Salini abound in the seventeenth-century inventories of noble Roman families [5], but the reconstruction of his *oeuvre* has been slow and beset with reversals. In the literature prior to 1964 (although retained in later editions of Charles Sterling's *Still Life Painting*), Tommaso Salini is credited with still lifes (monogrammed *ST*) demonstrably from the hand of Simone del Tintore (ca. 1630-1708) from Lucca. As a result, Salini was not even represented in the great *Natura Morta Italiana* exhibition in Naples in 1964. A single signed and dated still life of 1621 (Private collection, New York) (fig. 16) has been the touchstone for additions to Salini's *oeuvre* proposed by Mina Gregori and Federico Zeri [6]. This process of rediscovery is still in its first stage.

12. Boy with Flask

Oil on canvas. 99x73 cm.
Provenance: Salavin collection, Paris.
References: F. Zeri, 1976 (2), pp. 107-8, fig. 105.
Lugano, Baron H. H. Thyssen-Bornemisza Collection.

During the last decade of the sixteenth century in Rome, the development of still life painting was closely linked with the new taste for genre subjects (scenes observed from daily life) of the type of this *Boy with Flask* by Tommaso Salini. Although the earl sources do not credit Michelangelo da Caravaggio with the invention of such subjects, his examples of half-length figures *cu* still life were the most admired then, as now, and the most influential in Rome. It is worth noting in this context that in the 1607 inventory of paintings confiscated from the house of the Cavalier d'Arpino, several paintings of this format and unpretentious subject matter are cited, two of which have been plausibly identified with Caravaggio's *Bacchino malato* and *Boy with a Basket of Fruit* in the Galleria Borghese, Rome (figs. 11 an 12) [7]. The authors of the other genre pictures have not yet been identified; Pietro Paolo Bonzi [8] and Tommaso Salini are likely candidates. Prior to the publication by Federico Zeri of this *Boy with Flask*, only religious subjects and independent still lifes by Salini had been known. The excellence of the figure raised for Ze the possibility that Salini's contribution was confined to the cabbages that spill forward exuberantly. The young Michelange Cerquozzi was tentatively proposed as the collaborator responsible for the figure of the boy [9]. However, comparable faci types can be found in other works by Salini, as can parallels for th somewhat dry treatment of the figure — in contrast to the broadl painted still life. A date towards the end of Salini's career was pu forward by Zeri; in any event, the picture does not seem earlier than ca. 1610.

1) See W. Friedlaender, 1974, pp. 270-279, for an English transcription of the trial proceedings.

2) M. Gregori, 1973, p. 53 note 10.

3) See the list of Salini's *oeuvre* in B. Nicolson, 1979, p. 85.

4) G. Baglione, 1642, p. 288.

5) In November 1619 Tommaso Salini received 90 scudi from Cardinal Scipion Borghese as payment for "12 various paintings of flowers" destined for the villa Mondragone (P. Della Pergola, 1959, pp. 74-75, p. 220 no. 77). The 1627 inventory of the collection of Cardinal Francesco Maria del Monte refers to a "picture of flowers from the hand of Cavaliere Salina [sic] with a black frame, 3 palmi in size" (C. L. Frommel, 1971/72, p. 34). The Ludovisi collection of pictures contained almost fifty still lifes attributed to Salini in 1633, inventoried thusly: "Fifteen paintings depicting various vases of flowers... from the hand of Cav^e Tommaso [sic]"; "Another fifteen pictures of various vases of flowers... fro the hand of Cav^e Tommaso"; "Two small pictures of flowers... from the same hand"; "Another four pictures of vases of flowers... by the same"; "Two paintings depicting two parrots, one Red, the other green... by the same Cav^e Tommaso"; "Two paintings of fruits, four palmi in height and four and one-half palmi wide in a gilt frame, from the hand of the same"; "Eight small paintings of flowers from the hand of Cav^e Tomasso" (K. Garas, 1967, p. 344 nos. 72-77; no. 238). A pair of flower still lifes, reportedly bearing the signature(s) of Tommaso Salini were sold at auction in London in 1956, but are presently untraced (Christie's, 15 June 1956, lot 41, each 28 1/2x21 1/2").

6) M. Gregori, 1973, pp. 39-40, figs. 18, 19, 20; F. Zeri, 1976 (2), pp. 104-108

7) For more on this inventory, see under Exh. nos. 8 and 9, above.

8) A documented *Boy Holding a Melon* by P. P. Bonzi (ex-collection marchese Giustiniani) was destroyed in Berlin during the second World War (L. Salerno, 1960, p. 23, fig. 32).

9) F. Zeri, 1976 (2), pp. 107-108.

13. Still Life with Fruit and Game
Oil on canvas. 74x98.5 cm.
Unpublished.
Campione d'Italia, Silvano Lodi Collection.

Fig. 16. Tommaso Salini, Still Life, 1621. Private Collection, New York.

This unpublished *Still Life with Fruit and Game* can be safely
added to the corpus of still lifes by Tommaso Salini on the basis of
its correspondence in motif, palette, and brushwork with the
signed and dated *Still Life with Fruit* of 1621 (Private Collection,
New York) (fig. 16). The basket of mottled apples is closely
comparable not only to the basket in the signed example, but also
to a similar basket depicted in a painting of *Still Life with Fruit,
Vegetables and Crustaceans* (Ian Appleby collection, St. Helier,
Jersey, C.I.) that has been recently attributed to Tommaso Salini
by F. Zeri [1]. The painting in the Appleby collection also includes a
straw-wrapped wine flask that is reminiscent of the flasks found in
each of the pictures by Salini in the present exhibition.
With regard to the mouse and the snake (upper right and lower
left) in the still life dated 1621, Zeri rightly observed that Salini
was among the first artists to represent the " secret and silent life
of animals", thus anticipating the works of the North Europeans
Otto Marseus and Matthias Withoos, and of Paolo Porpora in
Naples [2]. The mixed depiction of both game and fruit in the
present still life from the Lodi collection brings to mind the
paintings of Salini's Flemish contemporary, Frans Snyders
(1579-1657). The influence of Snyders and of his pupil, Jan Fyt,
on the painting of such subjects in Italy during the second half of
the seventeenth century was profound. Snyders visited Italy
before 1609; prior to the establishment of the chronology of
Salini's still lifes, the nature of their exchange, if such it was,
cannot be determined [3].

1) F. Zeri, 1976 (2) fig. 104.
2) *Ibid.*, p. 106. A *Still Life* (St. Louis, City Art Museum) in which two mice
appear was signed and dated 1619 by Lodovico di Susio, a Netherlander active in
Turin and Rome.
3) A *Still Life with a Basket of Fruit* with Matthiesen Fine Art, London, (one of a
pair plausibly attributed to Salini) strikingly recalls Snyders's pictures of this
subject, even as regards the technique (London, 1981, no. 4, colorpls.).

Luca Forte
Active Naples, ca. 1625 - 1655

Bernardo De Dominici, author of the principal biographies of the Neapolitan artists (1742), had only disparaging words for Luca Forte. While he acknowledged Forte's precedence in the practice of still life, De Dominici was displeased by the severity of the artist's style: "If in his own time, [Luca Forte] was considered excellent in that kind of work [the painting of still lifes], at any rate he was poor in invention and in composition; one sees paintings by him... in which all the objects have been placed almost in a row, one after another in the same plane; very few works by this painter are seen that have items in the foreground and in the back."[1] Thanks to the investigations of Raffaello Causa during the past three decades, Luca Forte is appreciated today, *pace* De Dominici, as a worthy founder of the distinguished tradition of still life painting in Naples. Although regarded even in his own day as a specialist in still lifes of fruit[2], as more of his works are rediscovered, it is becoming apparent that he painted all the subjects typical of Neapolitan still lifes and that he was a primary influence on Giuseppe Recco and Giovan Battista Ruoppolo. He seems also to have been the first Neapolitan to paint still lifes with a landscape background[3].
Fortunately for posterity, Luca Forte was inclined to sign his paintings (but not to date them); otherwise his career is undocumented except for two letters that the artist sent in September of 1649 to Don Antonio Ruffo, an important collector in Messina. In one of these letters Forte mentions the prospect of a commission from Ruffo for a still life of "various fruits" for a fee of 200 ducats — an impressive sum of money[4].
According to Causa, Forte's career probably spanned three decades, from, roughly, the mid-1620's until into the 1650's[5]. The *Still Life with Fruit, Crystal Cups and a Tuberose* in the Galleria Corsini, Rome, was first recognized by Causa to be monogrammed *L F* in the twists of some vines and also an early work, on the basis of which Causa has assigned other pictures to the beginning of the artist's activity. Other signed or monogrammed paintings by the artist include the well-known *Still Life with Fruit and Flowers* in the collection of Maestro Molinari-Pradelli, Bologna (traced in some vines, *Luca Forte*) (fig. 19); an unusual *Still Life with Apples and Grapes*, on copper, with Galerie Meissner, Zürich, (*L F* in script) (fig. 17); the artist's most famous picture, the grand still life dedicated to "Don Joseph Carrafas" which has been lent to the present exhibition by the Ringling Museum, Sarasota (*L.F.* in block capitals) (Exh. no. 17). The Sarasota *Still Life with Fruit* was formerly in the collection of Mortimer Brandt, New York, with a pendant signed in full *Luca Forte F.* In 1972, E. Sestieri published a pair of flower paintings from a private collection, signed on the reverse, *Lucas Forte* (R.P. 26, 27)[6]. The mood in these two still lifes of flowers in vases is unusually Baroque for Forte, and might have appeased De Dominici had he only known them.

14. Still Life with Baskets of Fruit and Fish
Oil on canvas. 44.5x103 cm.
Reference: M. Marini, 1974, p. 326, fig. C55.
Campione d'Italia. Silvano Lodi Collection.

Although unsigned, the recently published attribution of this masterly *Still Life with Baskets of Fruit and Fish* to Luca Forte is fully convincing[7]. The painstaking brushwork, the polished surfaces of the fruits, and even the morphology of the not-quite-round apples are familiar parts of Forte's repertory. The yellow apples in the basket display another distinctive trait of the artist's technique, i.e. his tendency to paint lighter passages somewhat thinly, so that with time the darkly painted ground shows through underneath.
The comparison with Forte's signed *Still Life with Fruit, Crystal Cups and Tuberose* in the Galleria Corsini in Rome (fig. 18) brings forth two immediate observations, one for each of these two paintings. In the first place, it is striking how few of the hallmarks of Forte's characteristic style are noticeable in the Galleria Corsini *Still Life*, an early work: besides the dissolving quality of the chiaroscuro, only the pronounced geometry of the bursting pomegranate necessarily calls Luca Forte to mind. By contrast, the artist's habitual treatment of the fruit and the fisherman's tray in the still life in the collection of Silvano Lodi can be taken as evidence that the painting does not date as early in the artist's career as its strict Caravaggism would indicate. While the Galleria Corsini still life evinces an unambiguous dependence upon the initial responses in Rome to Caravaggio's conception of still life (the responses exemplified by such earnest, but inchoate paintings as nos. 8-10 in this exhibition), this *Still Life with Baskets of Fruit and Fish* represents a subsequent, direct assimilation by Luca Forte of Caravaggio's prototypes. The deliberate definition of a shallow space and even the selection of foodstuffs specifically evoke the table in a Caravaggesque *Supper at Emmaus*. Caravaggio liked to claim that the foundation of his art was his imitation of nature; Forte has understood in this extraordinary

Fig. 17. Luca Forte, Still Life with Apples and Grapes. *Galerie Meissner, Zürich.*

picture that the essence of Caravaggio's genius, however, was dramatic compression. As befits his later generation, Forte has instilled the movement of the nascent Baroque into his composition, but his arrangement is more remarkable for the isolation of the fruit and the fish in their halves of the picture. Considered together, this *Still Life with Baskets of Fruit and Fish* and the *Still Life with Fruit, Crystal Cups, and Tuberose* confirm in unmistakeable terms the determinant role of Caravaggio for the development of the Neapolitan school of still life painting, as R. Causa and C. Sterling have noted[8].

Prior to the publication of this still life depicting fish, only fruit and flowers were known from Luca Forte's brush, although an inventory of the collection of the principe di Scilla in Naples in 1747 refers to two pairs of paintings by Forte of poultry and other kitchen subjects[9]. In the present picture, the artist's selection of only three still life elements — apples, grapes and fish — naturally raises the question of a disguised symbolism. In fact, the most common symbolic meanings of these three items enact the central doctrine of Christianity when they are juxtaposed: the fated apple recalls the Fall and Original Sin, for which the Eucharist grapes represent the antidote provided by Christ, the Redeemer — whose symbol is the fish.

Fig. 18. Luca Forte, Still Life with Fruit, Crystal Cups and Tuberose. *Galleria Corsini, Rome.*

1) B. De Dominici, 1742, III, p. 293.

2) F. Baldinucci, 1975, VI appendix, p. 367, in a manuscript list, ca. 1676, of painters active in Naples after 1640, noted of him simply "Luca Forte painted fruits".

3) An attractive example, unsigned, is in the collection of Molinari-Pradelli, Bologna, see Naples, Palazzo Reale, 1964, no. 56, pl. 236. A pair of still lifes in landscapes, evidently by Forte, recently appeared on the auction market in New York, attributed to Paolo Porpora (Christie's, 9 January 1981, lot 101, colorpls).

4) V. Ruffo, 1916, I-II, pp. 58-61 (for both letters).

5) R. Causa, 1972, p. 1006.

6) E. Sestieri, 1972, p. 376f.

7) M. Marini, 1974, p. 326.

8) *Ibid.*, pp. 997-999; *idem*, 1978, p. 43; C. Sterling, 2nd revised ed. 1981, p. 87. R. Spear, 1975, p. 21, argues a contrary view.

9) See G. De Logu, 1962, p. 191.

5. Still Life with Cherries and other Fruits
il on canvas. 26.5x35 cm. (octagonal)
npublished
aples, Museo Duca di Martina (on deposit at the Museo
azionale di Capodimonte)

5. Still Life with Apples and Pears
il on canvas. 26.5x35 (octagonal)
npublished.
aples, Museo Duca di Martina (on deposit at the Museo
azionale di Capodimonte)

Fig. 19. Luca Forte, Still Life with Fruit and Flowers. *Molinari Pradelli Collection, Bologna.*

nese octagonal canvases of *Apples and Pears* and *Cherries and
her Fruits* were painted as pendants or possibly as two pictures
a more extensive series. They are among the earliest examples of
ill life paintings that are interrelated on account of their
ecorative values primarily, and not through their reference to a
ommon theme such as the Four Seasons or Attributes of the
irgin. This development — which opened the door to the
ivialization of still life painting in the hands of mediocre
ractitioners — seems to have been fostered by the artists of the
eneration born ca. 1600. Besides Luca Forte in Naples, Mario
uzzi (called " dei Fiori") in Rome (cf. R.P. 31-33) and the
inerant Giovanna Garzoni (active in Florence, Naples and
ome; cf. Exh. nos. 19-21) can be mentioned in this context [1].
iven Forte's miniaturist technique [2], it is surprising that more
ictures by him of small scale have not come to light. The motifs
nd the mostly yellow and red palette found in this pair of
anvases are recurrent features in his *oeuvre*. The signed *Still Life
ith Apples and Grapes* on copper (fig. 17) with the Galerie
leissner, Zürich, offers an apt comparison, especially as regards
ie palpable density of the fruits and their gem-like finish [3]. In the
osence of documentation, it cannot be judged as to which
oment in the artist's maturity these paintings date.

Tommaso Salini, the master of Mario dei Fiori, evidently also painted still lifes in
ecorative series. See note 5 under Exh. no. 12.
In a letter to Don Antonio Ruffo (V. Ruffo, 1916, I-II, pp. 58-61) Luca Forte
imself compares his technique to a miniaturist's, because of the tiny brushes he
ed.
See the previous entry, no. 14, for the possible symbolism of apples and grapes
presented together.

15

17. Still Life with Fruit

Oil on canvas. 78.9x104.7 cm.
Signed: *L.F.*
Provenance: Mortimer Brandt, New York, until 1961.
References: C. Sterling, 2nd revised ed. 1981, pp. 87 and 166 note 124, pl. 62; G. De Logu, 1962, p. 191; R. Causa, 1962, p. 43; S. Bottari, 1963 (2), p. 244, fig. 103b; Naples, Palazzo Reale, 1964, p. 41; R. Causa, 1972, p. 1007; P. Tomory, 1976, no. 154; M. Rosci, 1977, p. 98.
Sarasota, John and Mable Ringling Museum of Art.

In this major work from the last years of Luca Forte's career, the artist again indulges his penchant for "word-play". The canvas bears at its center a Latin dedication, *Don Joseph Carrafas*, which is rendered in the form of a string that one bird brings proudly to its mate. The patron in question, Don Giuseppe Carafa, was the unfortunate brother of the Duke of Maddaloni. During the Masaniello rebellion in Naples in 1647, Carafa was seized inside the church of Santa Maria La Nova, and lynched. It is difficult to construe the present picture as a memorial of that event, the date of which can be considered a definite *terminus ante quem*.
Raffaello Causa has characterized the Sarasota picture as a late work by Luca Forte, along with another signed still life in the Molinari Pradelli collection in Bologna (fig. 19), dated by Causa to ca. 1645-50 [1]. The late style of the artist is marked by his unflagging finesse for detail — in which respect the Sarasota *Still Life with Fruit* constitutes a *tour de force* — but also by his increasingly diffuse compositions. These were evidently this indefatigable master's response to the sense of lushness introduced into still life painting by the first full generation of Baroque artists, including Michelangelo Cerquozzi in Rome (R.P. 20) and Paolo Porpora in Naples (Exh. nos. 27-28). In Forte's last works, the dusky backgrounds seem to obscure or even consume some of the substance of the still life elements; the result is a singular translucence in these otherwise lapidary forms. This technique recurs in the still lifes of Giovan Battista Ruoppolo (cf. Exh. no. 29).

1) R. Causa, 1962, pp. 44 and 46; *idem*, 1972, p. 1007.

The cause of still life painting in Florence was advanced most effectively during the early seventeenth century not by a specialist, but by Jacopo Chimenti da Empoli, a noted painter of altarpieces and religious histories, who seems to have painted a few still lifes for his own amusement in the later years of his long life. Less than ten still lifes by Empoli are known, all of them are views of well-stocked larders. Two of Empoli's *Kitchen Scenes*, which entered the Galleria degli Uffizi as a pair in 1922, are signed and dated 1621 and 1624. Another dated example (1625) (fig. 20) and its pendant are in the Molinari Pradelli collection, Bologna. No particular preoccupation with still life details can be detected in the artist's vast production of figural compositions, but Empoli's style was distinguished from the first by his strict adherence to the passages of naturalism that he observed in the Florentine masters of the High Renaissance (through his master, Tommaso da San Friano, he traced his inspiration to Andrea del Sarto) and even of the Quattrocento. For want of a revolutionary presence of the kind of an Annibale Carracci or Michelangelo da Caravaggio, the Counter-Maniera impulses in Florentine paintings during the later sixteenth century were directed by artists who have been termed "reformers". Jacopo da Empoli learned much from the exercises in this spirit that Santi di Tito painted during the 1570's, and became in his turn one of the most influential "reformatori".

The earliest documented work by the artist is an altarpiece of 1579 now in the Louvre, Paris. The list of Empoli's altarpieces in every town in Tuscany and throughout Florence is too long to enumerate here. The artist kept a large studio and evidently enjoyed the interchange with his students, to judge from the escapades related by his biographer, Filippo Baldinucci. Empoli is perhaps most esteemed today for his gifts as a draftsman: his energetic drawings, invariably figure studies, can be found in every major collection.

18. Kitchen Scene

Oil on canvas. 119x152 cm.
Provenance: Giacomo Arbanasich (1922); Palazzo Pitti, Florence.
References: M. Marangoni, 1922/23 p. 480; S. DeVries, 1933, p 329; A. Venturi, 1933, p. 684; G. De Logu, 1962, pp. 85 and 18(pl. 43; M. Gregori, in Naples, Palazzo Reale, 1964, no. 157; M. Rosci, 1977, p. 100, fig. 78; S. Meloni Trkulja in *Gli Uffizi*, 1979-80, p. 259, P 581 (inv. 1890 no. 8441); C. Sterling, 2nd. re ed. 1981, p. 87.
Florence, Galleria degli Uffizi.

The obvious precedents for this *Kitchen Scene* dated 1624 and it pair dated 1621 (fig. 21) are the kitchen and market scenes painted at the end of the sixteenth century by Vincenzo Campi in Cremona (cf. Exh. nos. 1 and 2) and Bartolomeo Passarotti in

Fig. 20. Jacopo Chimenti da Empoli, Kitchen Scene. *Molinari Pradelli Collectio Bologna.*
Fig. 21. Jacopo Chimenti da Empoli, Kitchen Scene. *Galleria degli Uffizi, Floren*

Bologna (R.P. 4). The distinctions between Empoli's still lifes and those of the forebears just named are telling: Empoli has sharpened his focus on the individual foodstuffs to the point of eliminating participatory figures altogether. His interest is clearly not in genre subjects nor does there seem to be any allegorical content in his selection of fruits, vegetables, poultry and fish. Admittedly, the interpretation of Empoli's still lifes as passages of passionately faithful description is influenced by Baldinucci's biographical account of the artist[1]. The recurrent motif in Baldinucci's pages on Empoli is of the artist's enthusiastic appetites for food and drink. His patrons were encouraged to speed his hand with gifts of commestibles; so much so that a fellow artist, Jacopo Ligozzi, gave him the nick-name of "Empilo", the Italian word for "stuffed". Apropos perhaps of the succulent sausage that occupies the center of this *Kitchen Scene*, Baldinucci recounts a long anecdote about Empoli's workshop assistants and how they deceived their master by dusting the end of the sausage every time that they stole a slice. The seriousness and clarity (but not dryness) of Empoli's compositions, and of course the motifs, have been compared by Charles Sterling to the contemporary still lifes by the Spaniard Alejandro de Loarte[2]. The sources of this coincidence have yet to be explained. Although Empoli painted few still lifes, those that he did were created during a concentrated interval of time. They left their profound impress on the subsequent development of still life painting in Florence, so much so that the cool blue and green tonality favored by Empoli came to be typical of Florentine still lifes in general.

1) F. Baldinucci, ed. 1975, III, pp. 5-18, VII appendix pp. 24-27.
2) C. Sterling, 2nd rev. ed. 1981, p. 87.

The rediscovery of Giovanna Garzoni, miniaturist and still life specialist, was among the many contributions of the monumental exhibition of Italian still life paintings held in Naples in 1964. On that occasion, two pairs of octagonal still lifes in the Galleria degli Uffizi were identified by Mina Gregori with references to works by Garzoni in an inventory of the pictures extant in 1692 in the Medici Villa of Poggio Imperiale. With this basis of comparison, many other works have been convincingly attributed to Garzoni, most notably a group of twenty-six still lifes, likewise in tempera on parchment, in the Palazzo Pitti, Florence. Three examples from the Galleria Palatina collection have been lent to this present exhibition.

The outline of Giovanna Garzoni's career has been mostly reconstructed, although lacunae persist. No proper biography of her was compiled by a contemporary, but the few lines devoted to her life by Pascoli (1730) bear repetition here before a review of the documentation [1]. Garzoni left her native Ascoli in central Italy (the Marches) and became famous in various important cities for her " many beautiful and precious efforts "; however, she was especially appreciated in Florence, where she lived for a long time. Her pictures were so esteemed by the Florentine nobles and by the Grand Duke himself that she " sold them for whatever price she wished. " Pascoli concludes that Garzoni became rather rich, and retired in her old age to Rome.

It is assumed, but not documented, that Garzoni visited Florence at the start of her career, if she did not actually study there, because her style so clearly derives from that of Jacopo Ligozzi, a Veronese artist at the Medici court to whom Garzoni's works have often been misattributed. Ligozzi painted hundreds of illustrations of botannical and zoological specimens for Francesco de' Medici, who was an avid natural scientist. These works were conceived as lively extrapolations from nature and are considered to be the foundation of still life painting in Florence [2].

The earliest documentation of Giovanna Garzoni's activity, a signed and dated portrait miniature, places her in Venice in 1625 [3]. During this period of unknown duration in Venice the young artist composed a volume of calligraphic studies, now in the Accademia di San Luca, Rome, in which she noted that she was a pupil of a certain Giacomo Rogni [4].

By 1630 at least, Garzoni was an accomplished miniaturist, working and living independently. In February of that year she left Venice for Naples with a letter of introduction to the Duke of Alcalà [5]. From five letters sent between June of 1630 and July of 1631 to Cassiano dal Pozzo in Rome, we learn that Garzoni's talents found such favor with the Duke of Alcalà, that she had difficulty in fulfilling her commitments to her Roman patrons, namely dal Pozzo (a famous connoisseur) and Donna Anna Colonna, wife of Don Taddeo Barberini, prefect of Rome [6]. The subjects of the miniatures mentioned in these letters are various: a Head of St. John the Baptist, a Holy Family, and several " little portraits " (cartine di ritratti). By the definition of her day, the dimensions of a picture did not distinguish a " miniature " so much as the difficult and tedious technique of painting in tempera on parchment, the medium originally invented for manuscript illuminations.

After April 1631 and the recall to Spain of Alcalà, the artist's affection for Naples waned. Her only desire, she confided to dal Pozzo, was " to live and die in Rome. " However, she could not resist an invitation to enter in 1632 the service of Carlo Emanuele I, Duke of Savoy [7]. With the outbreak of war in 1637, Garzoni left Turin and seems to have settled in Rome, except for a documented sojourn in Florence, 1647-1649 [8]. Preserved in the archives of the Accademia di San Luca, Rome, is an account book of the artist's many works executed for the Grand Duke Fernando II and his brother Cardinal Giancarlo Medici and Prince Leopoldo Medici [9]. These included miniature portraits, copies of Madonnas by Raphael and Andrea del Sarto, and still lifes. For the Grand Duchess Garzoni painted several fans and a portrait of a lap dog, which she signed (fig. 23).

After 1654, the name of Giovanna Garzoni appears frequently in the records of the Accademia di San Luca, Rome; the date of her admittance into this society of artists is not recorded [10]. It was her wish to be buried in the Accademia's church of SS. Luca e Martina; towards this end she left her entire estate to the Accademia di S. Luca, including a valuable collection of drawings by old masters (Pascoli). Her funerary monument was not erected until 1698 and only through the initiative of Giuseppe Ghezzi, principe of the Accademia, who painted more than one portrait of her rather somber features [11].

19

19. Still Life with an Open Pomegranate
Tempera on parchment. 27x35 cm.
Provenance: Inv. 1890 no. 4759
Unpublished.
Florence, Palazzo Pitti, Galleria Palatina.

20. Still Life with a Bowl of Cherries
Tempera on parchment. 23x34 cm.
Provenance: Inv. 1890 no. 4764
References: Naples, Palazzo Reale, 1964, no. 15.
Florence, Palazzo Pitti, Galleria Palatina.

Although not strictly a pair, this *Still Life with an Open Pomegranate* and *Still Life with a Bowl of Cherries* both belong to a series of more than twenty still lifes by Giovanna Garzoni in the Palazzo Pitti, Florence. Typically these still lifes depict no more than one or two varieties of fruit or vegetable; together they comprise a decorative "gallery" of agrarian bounty and were quite probably commissioned for one of the Medici villas in the Tuscan countryside. The most ambitious piece in the group, *The Old Man of Artimino* (Exh. no. 21), was cited in a seventeenth-century inventory of pictures in the villa of Poggio Imperiale[12].

The considerable charm of Giovanna Garzoni's style, which she seems not to have modified significantly in the course of her career, derives from the adroit balance that the artist struck between archaisms learnt from Jacopo Ligozzi's sixteenth-century style of natural science illustration and her own gifts for decorative design. As Ligozzi did, so Garzoni preferred to paint her still life subjects in their actual dimensions with as much detail as her patience would allow. Ligozzi placed his specimens on blank backgrounds; the settings in Garzoni's still lifes are nearly as nondescript and probably more provocative by virtue of their extreme abstraction.

Garzoni borrowed these schemata from Ligozzi in the spirit of art, however, and not science. The most distinctive aspect of her technique, the stippling with the point of the brush, serves to undermine the objective clarity of her detailed vision in favor of a pictorial unity not found in Ligozzi. Moreover, her still life compositions are simple without being static. In the *Bowl of Cherries* the cherry stems point crazily in every direction; even without the use of such an energetic pattern, a sense of movement is imparted into the *Still Life with Open Pomegranate* by the compelling recession into space at the right-hand side.

Finally, Garzoni abandons the aims of science (and captivates her viewers) through her idiosyncratic manipulations of scale and perspective. The more interesting motifs in her still lifes are underscored, as it were, by inflated proportions. This non-naturalistic outlook must be a legacy of Garzoni's training as a miniaturist and appreciation for the ornamental borders in illuminated manuscripts. In both the *Still Life with Open Pomegranate* and the *Still Life with a Bowl of Cherries*, and in many other works by Garzoni, a peculiar system of perspective is at play. There is a pronounced sense in each of these compositions that the items in the center of the picture are the closest to the viewer and, concomitantly, that space falls back very quickly on all sides of this central point. The rather startling diminution of

Fig. 22. Giovanna Garzoni, Still Life with Two Melons. *Galleria Palatina, Palazzo Pitti. Florence.*

objects that are not truly so distant can be observed readily in a *Still Life with Two Melons* illustrated here (fig. 22) also from the Palazzo Pitti. These particular effects would seem to indicate that Garzoni made use of a convex mirror in the composition of many of her still lifes. Curved mirrors were a standard aid in every artist's studio of this period, so much so that they came to be regarded as emblems of the painter's profession[13].

1) L. Pascoli, 1730-1736, II. p. 451.

2) For Ligozzi, see Naples, Palazzo Reale, 1964, pp. 26-27; and Florence, 1961 [Mostra di disegni di Jacopo Ligozzi].

3) T. H. Colding, 1953, fig. 98.

4) A. Cipriani, 1976, p. 244 note 4.

5) *Ibid.*, p. 241. A. S. Harris and L. Nochlin, 1979, p. 136 note 13, refer to four works by Garzoni in the Biblioteca Nacional (nos. 7924-7927) presumably executed in Naples. A miniature by Garzoni of *Fruits and a Small Lizard* was in the collection of the Marques de Leganés, Madrid, in 1655 (S. Lopez Navio, 1962, p. 313 no. 1955).

6) S. Bottari, 1754/1783, I, pp. 342-348.

7) A. Cipriani, 1976, p. 241.

8) *Ibid.*, p. 241.

9) *Ibid.*, p. 244-245 note 11.

10) See A. S. Harris and L. Nochlin, 1979, p. 135 note 6, for documentation from the archives of the Accademia de San Luca. Contrary to the view of A. S. Harris, A. Cipriani (1976, p. 242) doubts that Garzoni was actually elected into the Accademia.

11) *L'Accademia Nazionale di San Luca*, 1974, p. 212 fig. 13, p. 227 note 19.

12) S. Meloni Trkulja, 1980, no. V, 15.

13) See H. Schwarz, 1952, pp. 97-118.

21. The Old Man of Artimino
Tempera on parchment. 38.6x60 cm.
Provenance: Donna Vittoria della Rovere, Villa of Poggio
Imperiale; Inv. 1890 no. 4778.
References: S. Meloni Trkulja, 1980, no. V, 15.
Florence, Palazzo Pitti, Galleria Palatina.

In size and subject, *The Old Man of Artimino* is an unusual
"miniature" from the brush of Giovanna Garzoni. The title is that
given to the picture in a seventeenth-century inventory of the
Medicean villa of Poggio Imperiale. Artimino was another
prominent Tuscan estate of the Medici, and it appears that
Garzoni has portrayed a faithful peasant in the act of bringing the
artist subjects for her still lifes, not to mention provisions for her
table. As composed by Garzoni with her predilection for
discrepancies of scale, this marvelous picture presents not one still
life but a variety of them, neatly laid out on a lunar landscape.
The dog who leans inward at the left as if to have his picture taken
reminds us that the villa of Poggio Imperiale was the favored
residence of the Grand Duchess Vittoria della Rovere, a great
fancier of dogs. The only miniature in the Galleria Palatina group
that is signed by Garzoni is a picture of a lap dog which was
commissioned by Donna Vittoria between 1646 and 1664 (fig. 23).

Fig. 23. Giovanna Garzoni, Portrait of a Lap Dog. *Galleria Palatina, Palazzo Pitti,
Florence.*

he life of Evaristo Baschenis appears to have been passed in an
mbient of quietude and reflection like unto that which we find in
s art. He was ordained a priest at an early age and is not known
• have ever resided outside of his native Bergamo in North Italy.
he suggestion by Francesco Maria Tassi (1793), his principal
ographer, that the young Baschenis must have studied with
nea Salmeggia, Giovan Paolo Cavagna or Francesco Zucco (the
ading Bergamasque painters of the pre-Baroque generation) is
• more than a prudent supposition. We know only that by 1647,
e career of *Prevarisco* ("Prete Evaristo") was sufficiently
dvanced for him to have in his workshop a competent replicator
*his designs (the anonymous *B.B.*), which were already in his
efinitive style.

the words of F. M. Tassi, "That in which [Baschenis] truly
icceeded was a most unusual manner that he himself invented,
hich was his alone and never used again by others: he painted
very sort of instrument of sound with incredible naturalness and
uth, and he succeeded in this with a perfection that I know has
ever been equaled." We would today add that Baschenis's
ompositions of musical instruments, like the *Oranges and
emons* of Zurbarán and the *Basket of Fruit* by Caravaggio,
chieve a level of artistic expression that transcends the
reconceptions associated with the category of "still life". Art
istorians are put into the uncomfortable role of poets when they
ndeavor to describe the ineffable and sometimes conflicting
ssociations of repose, optimism, melancholy and *memento mori*
1at arise from these images of superbly crafted instruments set
:op a table in studied disarray. From a poem written in his honor
uring his lifetime (1675) we learn that the works of Baschenis
ad already entered princely collections in Rome, Florence,
enice and Turin [1].

1 one respect, Tassi was not strictly accurate: Baschenis's
ompositions were never equaled in quality but they were
1assively imitated in kind. Marco Rosci has concluded that the
1aster himself oversaw the production by his atelier of repetitions
nd variants of his prototypes [2]. His manner was closely imitated
y his pupil Bartolomeo Bettera (1639(?) - post 1687) and less
ffectively by the latter's son, Bonaventura Bettera
1663(?) - post 1718) — and countless other local painters —
ith the result that the Bergamasque school poured out still lifes
f musical instruments (however diluted in effect) until well into
1e eighteenth century.

few still lifes of fruit and poultry by Baschenis have come down
) us. F. M. Tassi knew some small paintings by him of the
adonna and Child, which remain to be rediscovered.
resumably, the sacred subjects of Baschenis will be comparable
) those of his contemporary Carlo Ceresa (1609-1679), whose
fluence can be traced in the portraits that Baschenis painted in a
riptych of canvases for the Agliardi family, Bergamo (figs. 24, 25
nd 26). He portrayed himself, in fact, in the left-hand canvas of
nis triptych; two Agliardi nobles are shown with instruments in
1e right-hand canvas. The center-piece was reserved for a pure
till life.

Fig. 24. Evaristo Baschenis, Self-Portrait at a Spinet with Alessandro (?) Agliardi.
Agliardi Collection, Bergamo.
Fig. 25. Evaristo Baschenis, Bonifacio (?) and Ottavio (?) Agliardi. *Agliardi
Collection, Bergamo.*
Fig. 26. Evaristo Baschenis, Musical Instruments. *Agliardi Collection, Bergamo.*

22. Still Life with Musical Instruments and a Statuette
Oil on canvas. 87x115 cm.
Signed: EVARISTVS BASCHENIS F BERGON.
Provenance: Probably Conte Giacomo Marenzi, Torbiato
(Brescia); Legato Marenzi, 1926.
References: G. De Logu, 1931, p. 219, fig. 358; L. Angelini,
1946, p. 81, no. 2; M. Rosci, 1971, pp. 36, 43, 49, 55 note 15, fig.
1; M. Rosci, 1977, p. 101, fig. 86; F. Rossi, 1979, p. 259 no. 1390
(1138).
Bergamo, Accademia Carrara.

Musical instruments have been represented in art since antiquity;
by the mid-seventeenth century they had come to acquire in the
course of that journey an inordinate amount of symbolic baggage.
According to the context, musical instruments could be
understood as attributes of saints or references to profane love;
emblems of harmony, of the sense of hearing, or of the vanity of
human pleasures (the sweetest sound soon falls silent).
It is the "silence" of Baschenis's paintings that suggests his use of
musical instruments as protagonists in a *Vanitas* play.
Specifically, Baschenis conveys in his still lifes the sense of a
moment arrested in time. To the discomfiture of his interpretors,
Baschenis developed a personal idiom with minimal reference to
traditional iconography to express the central theme of the
Vanitas drama, which is that in time, everything on this earth —
crafted, cultivated or natural — must pass. As in this *Still Life with
Musical Instruments and a Statuette*, the curl of a page, the
shadow cast by a book are the artist's metaphors of temporality.
Although Dutch allegories of *Vanitas* are the likely antecedents
for the artist's still lifes of musical instruments, the ties are not
strong. Baschenis never painted an hourglass, a clock, a skull or a
guttering candle. (His followers did.)
Baschenis thus reveals himself as the spiritual heir of Caravaggio,
as has often been affirmed by scholars. Just as his fellow Lombard,
Baschenis organizes his images through chiaroscuro. Baschenis
suppresses the symbolic accoutrements in his still lifes as
Caravaggio eliminated the bystanders in his religious histories. In
the paintings of both artists, emotional tonality is expressed
through chromatic tonality.
F. M. Tassi (1793) made a pertinant observation, and a rare one,
in the art criticism of his day: "his works are esteemed in every
place not only by informed observers but even by every sort of
person, who, no matter how inexpert he may be, is taken by a great
pleasure and marvel by the sight of this artist's paintings, which
have a quality all their own."
Marco Rosci has compiled a list of still lifes by followers of
Baschenis that derive from the Accademia Carrara *Still Life with
Musical Instruments and a Statuette*[3]. The harp, the ink stand and
the lute in the center are constant elements in these other
compositions, but not the statuette. As it happens, Baschenis may
have intended a symbolic role for this statuette. In the midst of
attributes of literature and music, the statuette naturally brings to
mind the art of sculpture, raising the possibility that this still life
represents a *Vanity of the Arts*. Only the art of painting would be
absent from the allegory, and we can be certain that for Baschenis
it was emphatically present.

1) Bottari-Ticozzi, 4, 1822, pp. 22-23.
2) M. Rosci's 1971 monograph contains an unparalleled quantity of comparative
illustrations.
3) The group is considered "Series V" by M. Rosci, 1971, p. 43.

23. Still Life with Musical Instruments

Oil on canvas. 81x100 cm.
Signed: EVARISTVS BASCHEN
Provenance: Poletti Collection, Milan.
References: Finarte no. 4, March, 1963, no. 121; Naples, Palazzo
Reale, 1964, p. 62 no. 210, pl. 935; M. Rosci, 1971, pp. 51, 58
note 72, fig. 95.
Montreal, Private Collection.

This exhibition is privileged to include three paintings of musical
instruments by Evaristo Baschenis. Considered together, they
demonstrate an impressive variety of compositions. The majority
of the approximately eighty original works by Baschenis are
composed as horizontal rectangles. This *Still Life with Musical
Instruments* is nearly square in its format; in order to instill a sense
of movement amongst its elements, the artist has arranged them
along a steep diagonal [1].
Baschenis has no counterpart in European still life painting at
mid-century for his acutely non-decorative conception of the
genre and for his realization of a thematic profundity that is
usually exclusive to figure paintings. His paintings of musical
instruments are separated from the Northern European *Vanitas*
still lifes that probably inspired them by his injection of a
paradoxical development on the *Vanitas* theme. As in this still life,
the artist evokes the ephemerality of human existence through the
use of traditional symbols (a broken harp string, the disorderly
books, and of course the instruments themselves) and through
such personal metaphors of temporality as the shadow that
occupies center stage on the back of the mandoloncello, as well as
the crepuscular tonality. Imperious over the whole arrangement
sits a single burnished apple: a constant reminder of mankind's
Original Sin. Notwithstanding his Christian orthodoxy (and the
conventions of *Vanitas* still lifes), Baschenis nowhere intimates
that these superb instruments and cabinet are to be despised for
their " vain luxury. " For Baschenis, their impeccable
craftsmanship — although it cannot endure — is an affirmation of
the human worth that is not extinguished by Sin. They are heroic
accomplishments which Baschenis, like his English
contemporary, John Milton, acknowledges in man even after the
Fall.

1) This painting was exhibited with a pendant *Still Life* by Baschenis when in the
Poletti Collection, Milan (see references above for illustration).

24. Still Life with Musical Instruments

Oil on canvas. 98x145 cm.

Signed: EVARISTVS BASCHENIS F.

Provenance: Conte Moroni, Bergamo; Private Collection, Switzerland.

References: M. Biancale, 1912, p. 344; G. De Logu, 1931, p. 220; L. Angelini, 1946, p. 82, no. 17, pl. xiii; G. De Logu, 1962, p. 164; M. Rosci, 1971, pp. 41, 51, 55 note 22, fig. 103.

Campione d'Italia, Silvano Lodi Collection.

The familiar elements of the artist's vocabulary of form are in evidence in this grand *Still Life with a Spinet and other Musical Instruments:* to wit, the overlapping instruments that make a volumetric design in contrast to the planar pattern of the oriental rug; the piled books; and the restless pages of music. The dust that has settled on the curved back of the mandoloncello is another of the artist's emblems of Time. It is possible also that Baschenis intended a melancholic significance for this evidence of disuse of instruments associated with artistic inspiration.

This particular assortment of instruments with different ranges of tone suggests the actual setting of a *concertino* more than a majority of the artist's compositions. This impression is enhanced by the artist's suggestion of an actual room, the floor of which is glimpsed to the right. One imagines that Baschenis might have known his contemporary, Nicolo Amati, in nearby Cremona whose instruments he portrayed. Amati was the scion of the leading family of violinmakers in Cremona, and the master of Andrea Guarneri and Antonio Stradavari. Baschenis recognized that these men too produced timeless works.

25. Kitchen Scene
Oil on canvas. 53x120 cm.
Provenance: Canella collection, Milan.
References: M. Rosci, 1971, p. 52, fig. 83.
Private Collection.

Among the many paintings of musical instruments by Evaristo
Baschenis that were still in Bergamasque collections in 1793,
F. M. Tassi took particular notice of a still life of a different subject
matter — much like this *Kitchen Scene* — in the house of Conte
Giacopo Tassis in Borgo Sant'Antonio. "[Conte Tassis] has
among others a Baschenis painting with some dead birds and
other animals, also earthenware pots, copper pots, steel pots,
vegetables of every sort and other household articles such as are
seen in kitchens or larders."
In general, Baschenis's still lifes of fruit and poultry have been
considered early works; however, Marco Rosci has convincingly
related this *Kitchen Scene* to several similar *cucine* that can be
considered the master's last works in this genre. The artist's late
style, like that of so many masters, is marked by a striking
economy of touch and palette. Working almost in monochrome,
Baschenis seems to distinguish between the qualities of light that
his organic and metallic subjects emit, as opposed to reflect, from
the shadows. This is a kitchen still life that ignores the sense of
taste and touch. It is as if the artist has invented an iconography of
tonality; in place of the traditional symbols, the pensive half-light
makes of this image a *memento mori*.

5

After early studies with Daniele Crespi († 1630) in his native Milan, Pier Francesco Cittadini made his way to Bologna, where, at age seventeen, he entered the atelier of Guido Reni. The young *Milanese*, as he was called, soon distinguished himself for his adroit copies after the works of Reni and other Bolognese masters. In 1637 Cittadini painted the altarpiece of *The Stoning of St. Stephen*, his first recorded commission, for the prominent church of S. Stefano, Bologna. Prior to his prolonged visit to Rome, which was to be the turning point of his career, he placed other altarpieces in Bolognese churches, most notably a *Conversion of St. Paul*, S. Paolo, datable ca. 1641 [1].

C. C. Malvasia (1678) informs us that Cittadini was accompanied to Rome by a Flemish painter of landscapes in whose pictures Cittadini sometimes painted figures [2]. In Rome he was evidently struck by the proliferation of styles and genres being practiced by the international colony of artists. During the first half of the century, Bologna was without a school of still life painting with the partial exception of Paolo Antonio Barbieri in nearby Cento. The date of Cittadini's Roman sojourn has been estimated to ca. 1645 - ca. 1650 by E. Riccomini, who estimated a duration of at least a few years to judge from the radical transformation that took place in Cittadini's career [3].

In 1650-51 Cittadini was employed in collaboration with his brother, Carlo Cittadini, to paint fruit and festoons of flowers in the frescoed decoration of the Villa Estense in Sassuolo. Cittadini returned to Bologna (he was married there in 1653) a "universal painter" in Malvasia's description, which was not necessarily a compliment in the classicistic school of Bologna [4]. Besides painting still lifes of fruits and flowers, Cittadini now revealed his gift for portraiture, to which field he brought a (Lombard) clarity of vision and psychological insight unknown to contemporary Bolognese portraitists. The artist also painted landscapes with sacred or historical subjects which are alternatively reminiscent of P. F. Mola (in Rome) and of Francesco Albani, who had, however, little regard for the still life specialty of *Milanese* [5]. This resistance on the part of the Bolognese traditionalists did not deter the artist's considerable success, but was directly responsible for the scant mention he received in the contemporary literature on art. During his lifetime, paintings by Cittadini were collected abroad in Venice, Verona, Rome, Naples, and France [6]; Luigi Crespi (1769) concludes his brief biography of the artist with a rhetorical question: "In which house, in which palace in Bologna is there not some work of his?" In his own day, the most famous pictures by Cittadini were four allegorical canvases of *The Four Seasons*, which were described by L. Crespi in the collection of Count Legnani (now divided between the Museo Comunale, Bologna, and the Galleria Estense, Modena) [7]. In each painting, figural scenes appropriate to a particular season are represented within garlands composed of fruits and flowers from the same time of year. Similar kinds of decorative still lifes were perpetuated into the eighteenth century by the artist's three sons, who were also painters, and in turn by their sons [8].

26. Still Life of Fruit with Cat

Oil on canvas. 101x150 cm.
Provenance: Museo Coccopani.
References: G. Campori, 1855, p. 56 (as by Paolo Antonio Barbieri); G. J. Hoogewerff, 1924 (as by P. A. Barbieri); E. Riccomini in Parma, 1960-61, no. 83, pl. 112 (as by P. F. Cittadini); E. Riccomini, 1961, p. 368, pl. 1766; Naples, Palazzo Reale, 1964, no. 233, pl. 1066; M. Rosci, 1977, p. 183; R. Roli, 1977, p. 242.
Modena, Galleria Estense.

Two companion pieces to this *Still Life with a Cat* are also in the Galleria Estense, Modena, where all three paintings had been attributed to Paolo Antonio Barbieri until justly assigned to Pier Francesco Cittadini by E. Riccomini in 1960 and 1961. In the *Still Life with a Dog*, also set out-of-doors, a dog protects a table of fruit from a bird. The third picture of the series, a *Still Life with a Parrot*, depicts an interior with precious objects of glass and silver. A similarly exotic pendant for the *Still Life with Parrot* presumably once existed.

This *Still Life with a Cat* and the other still lifes that Pier Francesco Cittadini painted after his return to Bologna at mid-century reflect the artist's exposure to the "international Baroque" style of still life painting that emerged in the Roman school during the latter 1640's [9]. By that time, the naturalistic current associated with Caravaggio and his followers had been mostly submerged by the decorative and anecdotal sensibilities that an army of Northern European, especially Flemish, still life specialists had brought to Rome. As in this *Still Life with a Cat*, one of Cittadini's best known works, the introduction of episodes involving animals in the foreground and figures glimpsed in the distance is ultimately inspired by Flemish practice. Such anecdotes enliven the composition, but necessarily reduce the thematic importance of the still life elements. Cittadini's still lifes strike a personal and somewhat uneasy balance between their decorative yearnings and the artist's essentially naturalistic outlook, which can be traced to his Lombard heritage.

Fig. 27. Pier Francesco Cittadini, Still Life. *Museo Civico, Trieste.*

The depth of Cittadini's commitment to Roman Baroque modes
can be seen more readily perhaps in his *Still Life* in the museum in
Trieste (fig. 27), in which picture, by the way, the pair of melons in
the present *Still Life with a Cat* reappear. The unabashed
inclination towards ostentation in the Trieste picture is fully
characteristic of the "international Baroque" style of still lifes
that had recently been developed in Rome. Again, the sources are
to be found in North European still lifes, but the idiom was given
definitive form at roughly mid-century by the still shadowy figure
of Francesco Fieravino, called Il Maltese, (R.P. 24-25). In
Maltese's hands, the motif of a dish of biscuits and candies set
upon folds of an oriental carpet had been transformed into a kind
of password for unutterable luxury. Pier Francesco Cittadini and
other artists [10] who saw Maltese's still lifes in Rome during the late
1640's participated in the diffusion of this lavish vision, which left
its impression on artists as widely separated as Bartolomeo
Bettera in Bergamo and Giuseppe Recco in Naples (Exh. no. 31),
as well as in France and in North Europe.

1) This date is proposed by E. Riccomini, 1961, p. 364.

2) *Ibid.*, p. 365.

3) A. Arfelli, ed., 1961, p. 63.

4) C. C. Malvasia, ed., 1841, II. p. 178.

5) R. Roli, 1977, figs. 397 a-d.

6) M. Oretti, ms., cited by E. Riccomini, 1961, p. 362.

7) L. Crespi, 1769, p. 128.

8) R. Roli, 1977, figs. 400 a, c, d.

9) This designation of an "international Baroque" style of still life painting is
made by E. Riccomini, 1961, p. 368. In the opinion of the present writer, the key
personality of this moment is the mysterious Francesco Fieravino, Il Maltese.

10) Notably the Frenchman, Meiffren Conte, who was in Rome before 1651, and
derived his style from Maltese.

s early as 1742, when Bernardo De Dominici praised Paolo
orpora for — in essence — inducting the Baroque style into
eapolitan still life painting, authentic paintings by Porpora must
ave been as scarce as they are today. De Dominici describes
orpora's style in ringing tones but does not cite any specific
amples in Neapolitan collections, as he was wont to do. The
uvre of Porpora as it is known today is based on the researches
Raffaello Causa, who first published in 1951 several convincing
tributions to Porpora of still lifes that had previously passed
nder the name of Andrea Belvedere.
xcept for the dearth of signed works, Porpora's career is
asonably well-documented. On November 2nd, 1632, Paolo
orpora, age fifteen, was apprenticed to Giacomo Recco for a
eriod of three years [1]. Giacomo Recco, the father of Giuseppe
ecco, was among the first Neapolitan specialists in flower
aintings. De Dominici was under the impression that Porpora
ad been a student of Aniello Falcone, a painter of battle pictures
nd other figurative subjects. It cannot be ruled out that Porpora
as active for a period in the Falcone workshop as a still life
ecialist. Raffaello Causa has proposed Porpora as the author of
prominent passage of still life in a large *Concert* by Falcone in the
ado Museum, Madrid [2]. For the moment, however, no specific
otices regarding the artist's early career in Naples, other than the
aintings attributed to him, have come down to us.
orpora had left Naples permanently at least by February 1654,
e date of his marriage in Rome to a Anna de Amicis of Palermo [3].
September of 1655 he attended a *congregazione* of the
ccademia di San Luca in Rome and in the same year was listed as
new member in an internal memorandum of the Accademia [4].
is formal acceptance as an Academician took place on April
5th, 1656. Thanks to unpublished material from the archives of
e Accademia di S. Luca that Ann Sutherland Harris has kindly
ade available to this writer, we know that Porpora faithfully
tended *congregazioni* in each year (and usually more than one)
uring the period 1656-1670 with the exceptions of 1661 and
568 [5]. In 1666 Porpora received the honor of admittance into the
ongregazione dei Virtuosi al Pantheon, which society offered
asses for his soul upon his death in 1673 [6].
hat Porpora worked in Rome during the second half (at least) of
s career, explains satisfactorily the rarity of his still lifes in
aples, but makes even more mysterious the lack of impression
at he made in Rome. The slightly older Mario Nuzzi "dei Fiori"
noted by all of the commentators on painting in Rome at this
me — perhaps because he collaborated with leading figure
ainters. By contrast, neither Passeri (1673) nor Pascoli (1730)
ake any mention whatsoever of Paolo Porpora. P. A. Orlandi
704) had no information on the artist other than the date of his
ntrance into the Accademia di S. Luca. Yet, to have been
dmitted into the Virtuosi al Pantheon was a certain indication of
e respect borne him by his fellow artists. Several references to
ill lifes by Porpora in inventories of the Chigi collection in Rome
ave been pointed out by R. Causa [7]. Thus far, no other details of
e artist's patronage have been recovered.

27. Still Life with Flowers and Fruit

Oil on canvas. 98x129 cm.
References: R. Causa, 1951; G. De Logu, 1962, p. 190; Naples,
Palazzo Reale, 1964, no. 58, colorpl. IV; R. Causa, 1972, p. 1009,
colorplate; M. Rosci, 1977, p. 207.
Naples, Museo Nazionale di Capodimonte.

As De Dominici observed with some vehemence, the severe style
of still life that was prevalent early in the seventeenth century, and
exemplified in Naples by Luca Forte, was superseded in Naples by
the still life paintings of Paolo Porpora. "Paolo profited from that
which he had heard from good painters so as to increase the
beauty of his paintings... Leaving behind that dry mode of
composition [of Luca Forte], he began to make a copious
arrangement of delightful inventions, with a pictorial harmony
throughout; he augmented grace with natural observation, and
painted with the freshest colors; his paintings were marvelous of
their kind." [8]
The distinctions that De Dominici draws between Paolo Porpora
and Luca Forte are borne out by the comparison of this *Still Life
with Fruit and Flowers* with any of the several works by Luca Forte
included in this exhibition (Exh. nos. 14-17). The inalienable
merit of the still lifes of Luca Forte is not diminished by the
accomplishments of the next generation of artists, as De Dominici
would have it, but the sensuous textures and lush mingling of
colors in the Baroque style of the younger Porpora provided the
foundation for the mature styles of Giuseppe Recco and Giovan
Battista Ruoppolo, the archetypical Neapolitan masters of still
life.
As it happens, the influence of Luca Forte is clearly discernible in
this *Still Life* by Paolo Porpora. Many of the details, for example
the waxy leaves and some of the lilies, display sharp outlines and
hard surfaces that derive from the stony inventions of Forte.
Porpora adds certain elegances of motif and texture which
probably reflect the influence of Flemish still life specialists active
in Italy, especially Daniel Seghers in Rome, 1626-1627. However,
the naturalistic and optical basis of Porpora's art and of the
Neapolitan school in general (this too was the legacy of Luca
Forte) was sufficiently ingrained to be able to absorb the Flemish
lessons of selective description without compromise. These
flowers and fruits are as splendid as any painted in Rome or
Antwerp, and they have the qualities of organic forms, not silk
confections.

1) U. Prota-Giurleo, 1950, p. 12.
2) A. E. Perez-Sanchez, 1965, p. 389.
3) G. Ceci in *Thieme-Becker*, XXVIII, p. 273.
4) From an unpublished archival reference, Accademia di San Luca, Rome, made
available to me by Ann Sutherland Harris (see text).
5) G. Ceci, *op. cit.*, p. 273, had already referred to archival documentation for
Porpora's participation at the Accademia in the years 1656-1666. The
documentation discovered by A. S. Harris includes notices for 1667, 1669-70.
6) G. Ceci, *op. cit.*, p. 273.
7) R. Causa, 1972, p. 1009.
8) B. De Dominici, 1742, III, p. 293.

28. Still Life with Fruit, Flowers and Parrots
Oil on canvas. 95x131.5 cm.
References: R. Causa, 1951, pp. 31-33; G. De Logu, 1962, p.
190; R. Causa, 1972, p. 1009; M. Rosci, 1977, p. 104, fig. 89.
Naples, Museo Nazionale di Capodimonte (Inv. 296).

The most original aspect of Paolo Porpora's *oeuvre* are his
paintings of wildlife in natural settings. He can be said to have
painted animals with the accuracy of a zoologist but the soul of a
romantic poet. The Italian word for paintings that combine still
life and animal painting in this way is *sottobosco*, which has a
more provocative cadence than "underbrush".
Two Dutch artists who were active in Florence and in Rome at
mid-century, Otto Marseus and Matthias Withoos, are considered
the inventors of the detailed view of *sottobosco*. Porpora's
interpretation of the genre differs from these precedents in scope
and in profundity. In the works of Withoos, for example, the
viewer has the sensation of eavesdropping on the random activity
of assorted insects and amphibians, depicted with microscopic
clarity. In Porpora's paintings, such as this extravagant *Still Life
with Fruit, Flowers and Parrots*, the artist's vision of nature is writ
with the broad strokes of a novel as opposed to the specificity of a
textbook. As R. Causa has commented, Porpora employs effects
that range from "fortissimo to pianissimo, alternating violent
lights and romantic penumbrae."[1] Without
anthropomorphizing these wild cratures, Porpora makes their
responses and actions evocative of larger patterns of life. Some of
the animals in this *Still Life with Fruit, Flowers and Parrots* seem
to react to the sudden arrival of the viewer: the red parrot glares at
our approach, while another parrot on a branch above fixes a
quizzical gaze, a third bird departs. As a pair of crayfish scuttle
into their pool, a lizard is too intent on a butterfly to notice.

1) R. Causa, 1972, p. 1010.

To judge from the innumerable references to still lifes by Giovan Battista Ruoppolo in seventeenth-century inventories, the artist's name must have been synonymous with Neapolitan still life painting during his own lifetime. The principal biographer of the Neapolitan school, Bernardo De Dominici (1742) devoted separate chapters to only two still life specialists: Ruoppolo and Andrea Belvedere. Giuseppe Recco, Paolo Porpora, Abraham Breughel and the other seventeenth-century masters of still life are discussed under the heading of Ruoppolo's biography. De Dominici's deference to G. B. Ruoppolo underestimates the role of Giuseppe Recco however. As heads of rival schools during the second half of the century, Ruoppolo and Recco stood astride the frenetic production of still life painting in Naples like two Colossi. Nor were De Dominici's characterizations of Ruoppolo as the fruits specialist (grapes especially) and Recco as the fish specialist strictly accurate. Giuseppe Recco was the more universal personality, but G. B. Ruoppolo distinguished himself also in still lifes of flowers, game, and even fish.

The vital statistics of the artist are quickly told. His father was a painter of maiolica and probably responsible for his training. It is doubtful that Giovan Battista Ruoppolo studied with Paolo Porpora (as De Dominici maintained) since the latter was only a few years his senior. An elder brother, Carlo Ruoppolo, was also a painter, whose works are as yet unknown. The artist married in 1655, was the father of many children, and seems to have lived uninterruptedly in Naples for the entirety of his long life. A signed *Still Life with Flowers* in the Ashmolean Museum, Oxford, is considered by R. Causa to be an early example, datable ca. 1650, and inspired by the naturalism of Porpora (R.P. 46) [1]. The only dated painting by the artist is a *Still Life with Fruit and Bread* of 1661 in the Pinacoteca Comunale, Faenza.

In 1665 Giovan Battista Ruoppolo was listed as a founder of the first Neapolitan society of artists, the *Congregazione dei Santi Luca ed Anna*; he was elected to a term as *Prefetto* (titular head) in 1669, the only still life specialist so honored in his century. Among his many followers, the most familiar names are Giuseppe Ruoppolo (his nephew); Aniello Ascione; Francesco della Questa; and Onofrio Loth (R.P. 28). His compositions were models for generations to come.

29. Detail.

29. Still Life with Fruit
Oil on canvas. 180x125 cm.
Signed: ·G·B·Ruop.^{lo}
Unpublished.
Naples, Novelli Collection.

In the context of the present exhibition, this fully-signed *Still Life with Fruit* represents the culmination of the Caravaggesque current that was fostered in Naples by Luca Forte (Exh. no. 17) and adapted into the Baroque style of Paolo Porpora (Exh. no. 27). At each stage of this journey, these masters partook of parallel developments in Roman still life painting. From Luca Forte, Ruoppolo adopted his characteristic manner of composition in which a host of prominent motifs vie for the viewer's attention; Porpora demonstrated how to unify such arrangements by the interjection of movement. In Ruoppolo this sense of movement is accelerated thrice over and seems to lead in every direction at once. As in the late style of Luca Forte, the fruits seem to be composed as much of light as of water; Ruoppolo also borrows the insistent geometry of the pomegranates from Forte. Ruoppolo was heir to Paolo Porpora's seemingly contradictory concerns for both precise characterizations and exoticism. Both artists reveled in the extra-terrestrial oddity of the horny green squash (cf. Exh. no. 27). In the same spirit, Ruoppolo devoted the attention to distinguish three varieties of grapes, plus red apples, yellow apples, peaches, figs, quinces, and pomegranates. The cascades of grapes were a favorite motif of G. B. Ruoppolo, who very likely knew the similar treatments by Michelangelo Cerquozzi in Rome (cf. R.P. 20).
The proliferation of Ruoppolo still lifes such as the present painting and also the high value placed on them by contemporaries is evidenced by two entries in an inventory compiled by Luca Giordano in 1688 of the collection of Don Giuliano Colonna in Naples. Among seven still lifes attributed to G. B. Ruoppolo, Giordano described two of similar format, a *Fruits and Flowers with Half-Watermelon* valued at 50 lire and a "painting of bunches of grapes, pomegranates, and melons" valued at 40 lire[2]. Equivalent valuations were assigned to a landscape by Giovanni Benedetto Castligione, a *St. Margaret* by Bernardo Cavallino and a *Magdalen* by Luca Giordano himself.

1) Naples, Palazzo Reale, 1964, no. 78.
2) F. Colonna, 1895, nos. 58 and 82.

30. Still Life with Crab and Fish
Oil on canvas. 98x149 cm.
Unpublished.
Naples, Pagano Collection.

Giovan Battista Ruoppolo's achievements as a painter of still lifes
of fish have been rediscovered by modern scholarship. Under the
influence of the writings of Bernardo De Dominici (1742), this
field was believed for centuries to be the exclusive province of
Giuseppe Recco who, admittedly, painted many more marine still
lifes. The attribution of this unsigned *Still Life with Crab and Fish*
to Ruoppolo is confirmed by comparison with the artist's *Still Life
with Fish* in the Museo di San Martino, Naples (signed *G. B.
Ruoppolo*) (fig. 28) [1]. In contradistinction to Recco, Ruoppolo's
compositions — whatever their subject matter — seem to evolve
organically from the individual volume and colors of the still life
elements. Ruoppolo takes particular delight in giving definition to
the most complicated conglomerations of masses, and he enriches
the mixture with his sensuous conception of texture. Recco, by
contrast, has a more intellectual approach to picture-making even
at his most spontaneous (e.g. Exh. no. 32, but cf. Exh. no. 33). The
comments of Raffaello Causa with regard to Ruoppolo's *Still Life
with Fish* in the Museo di San Martino apply as well to the present
example: as opposed to the studiously balanced and clarified
images of Recco, "Giovan Battista Ruoppolo evinces an
immediacy, a frank spontaneity of vision that excludes any
indulgence in compositional definition and which lends itself to a
rapid and brilliant pictorialism." [2].

Fig. 28. Giovan Battista Ruoppolo, Still Life with Fish. *Museo Nazionale di San
Martino, Naples.*

1) This comparison was made by F. Bologna in a letter of 20 February 1979.
2) Naples, Palazzo Reale, 1964, no. 84.

Giuseppe Recco was the most famous member of a family of still life specialists. Giacomo Recco, his father, painted some of the first still lifes of flowers in Naples, and was the master of Paolo Porpora. Slightly older than Giuseppe was his uncle (or perhaps his elder brother), Giovan Battista Recco, whose career is not well-documented but who appears to have represented a "Spanish" tendency in the Neapolitan school. A few kitchen scenes and still lifes of fish by G. B. Recco, dated or datable to the 1650's, reveal a cultivated sensibility for intimacy and reserve. In recent years, major advances have been made in the effort to distinguish the works of Giuseppe Recco from those of his relatives and rivals (Giovan Battista and Giuseppe Ruoppolo) with the same monogram, *G.R.* Fortunately for the purposes of scholarship, one of the most characteristic manifestations of Recco's individuality was his inclination to sign and date his works. The prominence and frequency of Recco's signatures beg some discussion of them. It is not possible to date his works according to the variant forms of his signature, as A. E. Pérez-Sánchez has attempted [1], save that the prefix *Eques* (knight) does not appear earlier than a *Still Life* of 1680 in the Pinacoteca Comunale, Pesaro. In addition to an unpublished *Marine Still Life with Fisherman*, 1668, in this exhibition, the signed and dated works by Giuseppe Recco are: a *Still Life with Moor* of 1659 (Medinacoeli Collection, Madrid); a *Still Life with Fish*, dated 1664, previously attributed to G. B. Recco (Moret Collection, Madrid) [2]; a large *Marine Still Life with Boat*, 1666 (Private Collection, Naples); an unfinished *Still Life with Fruit, Flowers and Birds* of 1672 (Capodimonte, Naples); *The Fish Vendor's Stall*, 1674 (Gaudioso Collection, Catania); *Kitchen Scene*, 1675, (Akademie, Vienna); *The Five Senses*, 1676 (Private Collection); a *Kitchen Still Life* dated 1679 (at Christie's, London, 15 October 1970); a pair of monumental *Vases with Flowers* one dated 1683, the other documented 1684 [3] (Marquess of Exeter, Burghley House); *Still Life with Fish* of 1691 (Uffizi, Florence).
In a sense the diverse works of art listed above constitute the vital statistics of Giuseppe Recco's life. After an early marriage in 1654, he seems not to have travelled outside of Naples. In 1665 he was alongside his rival, Giovan Battista Ruoppolo, as a founder of the *Congregazione dei Santi Luca ed Anna*, a professional society of Neapolitan artists. The date and circumstances of his knighthood have not yet been recovered; De Dominici offers an extended, but mendacious account of it. From the same source, it appears that Recco died of a fever in 1695 in the Spanish port of Alicante. At this unlikely moment of his life, he seems to have accepted the invitation of Carlos II to serve the Spanish court. His closest followers were his son and daughter, Nicola Maria Recco and Elena Recco. The most sensitive interpretor of his style was Andrea Belvedere.

31. Still Life with Violin and Sweetmeats on a Table
Oil on canvas. 119.4x161.3 cm.
Signed: GR [in the violin string].
Unpublished.
England, Private Collection.

The artist has traced his monogram *G R* in the violin string that dangles over the edge of the table. He could hardly have known that three hundred years later this stroke of whimsy would prove a blessing to scholarship. Without this signature, the attribution of this *Still Life with Violin and Sweetmeats on a Table* to Giuseppe Recco would undoubtedly be controversial, given that the school of Naples was in the main a bastion of resistance against the taste for splendor in Baroque still lifes. With respect to motif and format this sumptuous picture relates directly to one of the most important developments in Roman still life painting in the mid-seventeenth century, namely the similarly grand compositions by Francesco Fieravino, Il Maltese (R.P. 24-25). The demand for these emblems of luxury proved to be international, and as it happens, the prominence of the silver-gilt ewer in the present *Still Life* by Recco specifically recalls the work of Meiffren Conte, a French imitator of Maltese, known to have been in Rome in 1651 [4].
Were this patently Roman conception not graced with the monogram of Giuseppe Recco, his authorship would nonetheless be demonstrated by three separate considerations, the foremost being the distinctively Neapolitan technique of the painting. Forms and texture are defined through a sharply-focussed chiaroscuro. Secondly, the "flower still life" that rests upon the magnificent carpet clearly pertains to the late works by Giacomo Recco. A comparable vase of flowers was published by R. Causa in his fundamental study of the artist [5]. Finally, the name of Giuseppe Recco inevitably comes to mind, as he was the only Neapolitan master known to have taken an interest in the Roman innovations of Maltese. Recco's most noted painting in this genre is the signed *Still Life with Masks and Musical Instruments* in the Boymans-van Beuningen Museum, Rotterdam [6]. Bernardo De Dominici, writing in 1742, mentions still lifes of sweets as a specialty of the artist [7], and several signed examples have been identified. Moreover, De Dominici supposed (although he presented his supposition as fact) that the non-Neapolitan influences on Recco must have been the result of studies in Milan, "before the age of twenty." [8] In fact, had Recco been in Lombardy ca. 1650 he would not have seen any still lifes in the style of Maltese unless they had been imported from Rome.
Several factors indicate a date at the very beginning of the artist's career for this picture, possibly prior to 1654 and the death of his father. To return to the signature, Giuseppe Recco is only known to have signed early works in an improvised manner (imitative of Luca Forte); he seems soon to have settled on block letters. The treatment of the flowers is so tied to our understanding of Giacomo Recco's late style, that Giuseppe could conceivably have painted them with the guidance of his father. The particular qualities of the hand and eye of Giuseppe Recco are unmistakeable in the composition as a whole, however, wherein the exuberance of the individual elements (imagine such a platter of biscuits!) is moderated by the subtle symmetry of the design.

1) A. E. Perez-Sanchez, 1965, pp. 423-424.

2) The attribution to Giuseppe has been restored by R. Causa, 1972, p. 1021.

3) A photograph of one of this pair by Giuseppe Recco is here published (R.P. 41). According to the Marchioness of Exeter *Catalogue of Pictures at Burghley House*, 1954, the painting with the two figures bears the date 1683. These paintings were commissioned directly from the artist by a George Davies on behalf of " the Conte di Exeter ". A bank document of 10 May 1684, published by G. B. D'Addosio, 1913, p. 493, reveals that the fee for the " two pictures of flowers " (palmi 10 by 8) was agreed at 200 ducats each; one of the pictures had already been painted by this date, and the other was to be finished within the month. No mention is made of the collaboration of a figure painter, and in fact the figure style accords with the few known examples by Recco himself.

4) M. Faré, 1974, p. 208; cf. the illustration (Coll. Seghers), p. 209, especially.

5) R. Causa, 1961, p. 349, pl. 156a.

6) Naples, Palazzo Reale, 1964, no. 63, pl. 27a. First published by F. Zeri in 1952, who noted the signature, *G. Recco*. R. Causa, 1972, p. 1050 note 6, remarks that the initial letter is illegible.

7) B. De Dominici, 1742, III, pp. 295, 297.

8) *Ibid.*, p. 295. R. Causa, 1971, pp. 1022-23, has refuted the possibility of an apprenticeship in Lombardy, and remarked instead on the influence of Maltese. F. Bologna, 1968, under no. 45, reports the existence of a pair of still lifes of fruits and vases by Giuseppe Recco with signatures traced in grape vines: *G.R.* and *Giuseppe pisquillo* [greenhorn].

32. A Kitchen Interior with a Still Life of Fish

Oil on canvas. 121.5x175 cm.
Signed: *Gio·ᵉ Recco F.*
References: London, 1981, no. 14, colorpl.; London, 1982, no. 115.
London, Matthiesen Fine Art Ltd.

Giuseppe Recco stands out within the context of High Baroque still life painting for his capacity to reconcile the humble subjects and naturalistic bias of the Neapolitan school with an innate sens of formal balance that can only be termed " classicistic. " This *Kitchen Interior with Still Life of Fish* makes its immediate impression for its multiplicity of glistening tones, the intensities c which are heightened by the contrast with the neutral values of th interior space. It is typical of Recco to unify the backdrops of his still lifes to allow a profusion of motifs without sacrifice of clarity The " classical " quality of Recco's vision lies in the underpinning of symmetry and regulated movement that give order to his seemingly casual compositions. In this *Kitchen Interior*, nearly al of the color occurs in a single foreground plane; it is surprising to note the measured cadence with which these color accents descend a series of steps from right to left. The triple-hooked gaff with its symmetrical catch of two fish and a ray (behind), was placed in this same foreground plane and given dramatic prominence by its precise centering.

Carlo Volpe has noted the influence of Giovan Battista Recco in this still life by the younger Giuseppe and thus proposed a relatively early date of ca. 1660 for its execution [1]. Both of these observations are warrented by our present understanding of thes artists' *oeuvres*. The still lifes of Giovan Battista Recco were the most likely source for Giuseppe's mode of compositional restraint. It is notable, however, that Giuseppe Recco inherited none of the Spanish-influenced quality of *sosiego* (tranquility) that distinguishes his uncle's paintings. In Giuseppe's still lifes th tautness of the pictorial structure more readily evokes a sense of disquiet than of pervasive calm.

1) London, 1981, no. 14.

33. Marine Still Life with Fisherman
Oil on canvas. 180x230 cm.
Signed: *G·ᵉ Recco 1668.*
Unpublished.
Naples, Pagano Collection.

This *Marine Still Life with Fisherman* resounds with all the *joie de vivre* and enthusiasm of a Neapolitan folk song. The size and improbable variety of this fisherman's catch make this picture a cornucopia of fish as well as a celebration of Neapolitan seamanship.
By a fortunate circumstance, this major example of Neapolitan Baroque still life painting is not only signed and dated by the artist, but even the details of its commission are known to us. Ferdinando Bologna has identified this unpublished canvas by Recco with a painting mentioned in a bank document of 1669, which was discovered and transcribed by G. B. D'Addosio in an article of 1913 [1]. From this document, which records a payment by Giacomo Paravagna, Marchese di Noja, to Giuseppe Recco of twenty ducats on account of a fee of 100 ducats for a painting 9x7 palmi in size, of various kinds of fishes " with a figure of a fisherman by Luca Giordano. " [2] By virtue of this last consideration the *Marine Still Life with Fisherman* thus qualifies as an important addition to the *oeuvres* of two artists, not one. The fisherman in this painting is unmistakably from the brush of Luca Giordano. Bernardo De Dominici had referred to collaborations between Giordano, the leading artist in Naples during this period, and Giuseppe Recco; the present example is the first such work that has been rediscovered [3]. The discovery of the bank document, moreover, sheds much light on the prestige of still life painting in Naples during the second half of the seventeenth century: the commission for the painting was awarded to the still life specialist, Giuseppe Recco, who sub-contracted the figure portion of it to Luca Giordano, who evidently did not find his subsidiary role demeaning.

1) G. B. D'Addosio, 1913, p. 493. Prof. Bologna will discuss this painting in depth in a forthcoming article on collaborations between still life specialists and figure painters.
2) The specific transaction recorded in this document is the authorization by the Marchese di Noja of payment of 20 ducats to the artist to make a total of 62 paid towards the full price; the painting was to be delivered within two months. The discrepancy in date from that of 1668 inscribed by Recco on the painting itself is probably due to the lapse of time required to accomodate the collaboration of Giordano. Avv. Paolo E. Pagano kindly provided me with a full transcript of this document. One *palmo* is roughly equivalent to 23 cm.
3) B. De Dominici, 1742, III, p. 296. Luca Giordano is reported to have painted fishermen in two large canvases with fish by Recco that were included in an exhibition of 14 still life paintings organized by Giordano during the festival of *Corpus Domini*.

Abraham Brueghel
Antwerp 1631 - 1697 Naples

Of all the European artists who made their way to Italy during the seventeenth century to study at the fountainhead of art, the still life and the landscape painters of Flanders demonstrated a nonpareil capacity to assimilate the native culture and to enter the mainstream of Italian society. This phenomenon was exemplified in its every detail by the career of Abraham Brueghel, whose participation in the development of Italian Baroque still life painting justifies his inclusion in this exhibition.

Abraham Brueghel was born in Antwerp, the son of Jan Brueghel II; it was his fate to be the last distinguished representative of the artistic dynasty founded a century before by Pieter Brueghel the Elder. His grandfather, Jan Brueghel *de Velours*, had worked in Naples, Rome, and especially Milan at the turn of the century, and was among the artists who gave definitive form to the independent genres of flower paintings and landscapes. Abraham entered the painters' guild in Antwerp in 1655, but no works from his pre-Italian career have been identified. By 1659 he was already resident on the via del Babuino in the artists' quarter of Rome. His principal influences were the increasingly lush styles of three Flemish forerunners, who had also worked in Italy: Frans Snyders, Jan Fyt, and Pieter Boel. Onto his native predilection for decorative profusion and anecdote, Brueghel seamlessly grafted the sweeping movement of the High Baroque still lifes of Michelangelo Pace da Campidoglio.

Rome was the center of Brueghel's activity for at least a decade, during the course of which he visited Messina twice, in 1663-64 and 1667-68, in order to meet with his most important patron, Don Antonio Ruffo. Brueghel's letters to Ruffo in the years 1665-1671 are preserved and are as valuable for their first-hand description of the Roman art world during those years as for their information on the artist's activities [1]. With his comfortable command of Italian, Brueghel writes amiably of his efforts to acquire paintings for the Ruffo collection, of the reputations of the leading artists of the day, and of toasting the health of Don Antonio with his friend and neighbor Claude Lorrain. Brueghel relates that he has painted still lifes with figures by Giacinto Brandi and G. B. Gaulli (1666). He is also known to have collaborated with Carlo Maratti, the leading painter in Rome, and with Guglielmo Cortese. In 1670, Breughel was admitted into the Accademia di San Luca, Rome. The earliest dated painting by Abraham Brueghel is a still life in the Rijksmuseum, Amsterdam, signed *A Breughel F. Roma 1670*. The orthography of the artist's numerous signatures varies somewhat, but not nearly so much as in contemporary Italian texts (*Brugolo, Bruchel, Brugora, Bruguero, Brucolo*, etc.). Brueghel was honored with admission into the Congregazione dei Virtuosi al Pantheon in 1671. His presence in Rome is recorded for the last time on September 17, 1673 [2]. The Neapolitan period of Abraham Brueghel's career had begun by 1675, in which year a son was born to him (and his Roman wife) in that city. Bernardo De Dominici (1742) writes admiringly that Brueghel was "famosissimo" for the ease with which he composed grand canvases of fruits and flowers arranged about monumental vases and such motifs. His works were esteemed by the *caposcuola*, Luca Giordano, and could be seen in many noble houses. Brueghel's arrival in Naples signalled the definitive introduction into the local school of the completely decorative mode of still life painting that had evolved by that date in Rome, largely through his own efforts.

34. Still Life in a Landscape
Oil on canvas. 122.2x160.6 cm.
References: O. Ferrari and G. Scavizzi, 1966, II, p. 308 (figure by Giordano); S. Ostrow, 1968, no. 37; D. Bodart, 1970, I, p. 49 R. Causa, 1972, p. 1046 note 77; D. Graf and E. Schleier, 1973. pp. 55, 57 note 37, fig. 10 (figure by S. Ricci).

Providence, Museum of Art, Rhode Island School of Design.

Due to the relative constancy of the artist's mature style and the scarcity of dated works, the chronology of Brueghel's *oeuvre* has thus far resisted solution. At first sight, the figure in this *Still Life in a Landscape* would seem to indicate a date towards the end of the artist's career in Naples. Brueghel's responsibility for the fruit in this still life has been accepted by every commentator on the picture; after unconvincing attempts to recognize the hand of Luca Giordano in the half-length figure of the country girl, Dieter Graf and Erich Schleier were undoubtedly correct in their attribution to Sebastiano Ricci. As a young painter from Venice, Ricci studied in Rome during the years 1691-93. However, it was discovered in the course of recent restoration that Brueghel must have been an unwitting collaborator with Ricci. Radiographs have confirmed that Ricci's figure of a girl was painted over a figure of seated boy, the work of another artist. What is more, the pudgy features of this boy, who, sitting cross-legged, reached up with his left arm to take some grapes from the nearest bunch, are sufficiently clear in the x-ray to allow the observation that this earlier painter was not a Neapolitan, rather a Roman, possibly Guglielmo Cortese. Brueghel is known to have painted still lifes in collaboration with Cortese, Giacinto Brandi, G. B. Gaulli, and other figure painters in Rome during the 1660's. This *Still Life in Landscape* from Providence appears therefore to be a masterpiece from the early maturity of Brueghel which has been enhanced, perhaps ca. 1700, by a contribution from Sebastiano Ricci, acting no doubt, upon the instructions of a collector.

In comparison to the still lifes of his Neapolitan contemporaries, Giovan Battista Ruoppolo and Giuseppe Recco, Abraham Brueghel's compositions appear to have been conceived with remarkable casualness. Despite the abundance of detail in his fruits and other motifs, they are at heart generalizations that are more like superb counterfeits — again by comparison to the Neapolitans — rather than the real thing. De Dominici summed up the differences between the styles of Brueghel and Ruoppolo in a passage that invites quotation: "Certainly if Gio: Battista Ruoppoli had had the imagination (*bizzarria*) for composition of Brueghel joined to the great study that he made of everything from life, he would have been miraculous. But Brueghel was so extravagant, that he used to take a rather large watermelon and, dropping it on the ground, would paint it broken, exactly as it remained from its fall. He would then add other fruits about it and other accompaniments in order to complete the beautiful ensemble of his picture, which came from his hand with supreme grace and the most spirited painting." [3]

1) V. Ruffo, 1916, pp. 172-188.
2) According to an unpublished reference from the archives of the Accademia di San Luca, Brueghel attended a meeting on this date. I am grateful to Ann Sutherland Harris for this information.
3) B. De Dominici, 1742, III, p. 298.

Very few particulars about the life of Antonio Maria Vassallo have come down to us, undoubtedly because he seems to have died when still a young man [1]. Vassallo was a pupil of Vincent Malò, a Fleming who arrived in Genoa from Antwerp in 1634. His earliest lessons were therefore absorbed undiluted from the workshop of Peter Paul Rubens; the few religious compositions that have been securely attributed to Vassallo are assumed to be relatively early works on account of their strict adherence to Rubensian models. Among these pictures is the *Four Saints* (a fragment) of 1649, his only dated painting, in S. Girolamo, Quarto. G. V. Castelnovi (1971) has pointed out, however, that two lunettes in the chapel of the Madonna del Carmine, S. Anna, Genoa, were probably painted at the time of the chapel renovation in 1654.

It is clear in any event that Vassallo gradually shed his initial Rubenism and moved into the sphere of Giovanni Benedetto Castiglione, who returned to Genoa and was active during the 1640's. Several pastoral subjects by Vassallo in the manner of Castiglione have been identified.

Vassallo's production of still life paintings has only in the present century been recovered from its early assimilation into the traditional *oeuvre* of G. B. Castiglione. In an article of 1923, O. Grosso published his discovery of Vassallo's signature on one of a pair of large animal/mythological subjects in the Hermitage, Leningrad [2]. The paintings in question, a *Nurture of Cyrus* and an *Orpheus*, had been attributed to Castiglione since the early eighteenth century. Thanks to Vassallo's economical practice of reusing favorite motifs in various arrangements from picture to picture, it has been possible to enlarge his *oeuvre* considerably. In the process, Vassallo has emerged as a still life specialist of substantial relief. A comprehensive list of current attributions to the artist is given by P. Torriti [3]. De Logu has remarked on the importance of Vassallo for Giovanni Agostino Cassano (ca. 1658-1720), the most noted painter of still lifes in the Genoese school.

35. The Larder

Oil on canvas. 229x163.2 cm.
Provenance: Cardinal Joseph Fesch, Rome (sale, 1845, as Castiglione); Reginald Cholmondeley, Condover Hall (sale, Christie's, London, 6 March 1897, no. 66 as Velázquez); Cook Collection, Richmond, Surrey (catalogue 1903, no. 29, attr. Velázquez; catalogue 1915, III, no. 504, attr. Spanish school; catalogue 1932, no. 504, Castiglione); Contini Bonacossi, Florence (sold 1949 to the following); Samuel H. Kress Collection, 1961.
References: C. B. Curtis, 1883, p. 36 (attr. Velázquez); T. Borenius, 1913, p. 17 (attr. Murillo); A. L. Mayer, 1915, p. 126 (attr. Mariano Nani); R. Longhi, 1950, p. 39 (Vassallo); G. De Logu, 1962, p. 48; Naples, Palazzo Reale, 1964, p. 108; P. Torri 1971, II, pp. 335, 338; F. R. Shapley, 1973, p. 93 (K1635); M. Rosci, 1977, pp. 107, 168 note 111, 238, pl. 33; F. R. Shapley, 1979, p. 516 (1643); C. Sterling, 2nd rev. ed. 1981, p. 87.
Washington, D.C., The National Gallery of Art.

Long attributed to Giovanni Benedetto Castiglione and then briefly, at the end of the nineteenth century, to Diego Velázquez, *The Larder* was first recognized as a masterpiece by Antonio Maria Vassallo in 1948 by Roberto Longhi, who published his attribution in 1950. As more still lifes by Vassallo have come to light, *The Larder* has been revealed as a compendium of the artist's favorite motifs. For instance, the hen at lower left reappears in one of the Hermitage pictures and in other, smaller still lifes by Vassallo, as F. R. Shapley has observed [4]. Without citing every such repetition, it is worth noting that the peacock in *The Larder* recurs in a painting of *Animals* (Private Collection, Genoa) [5] which was attributed to G. B. Castiglione in the Palazzo Bianco exhibition of Genoese paintings in 1969; Ann Percy proposed thereafter an attribution to Vassallo [6]. The miracle is that the artist was able to repeat his still life elements as often as h did, while avoiding any sense of repetitiveness in his composition (only a certain *deja vù*).

The eighteenth-century attribution to Castiglione of *The Larder* was to be expected given the obscurity into which Vassallo's reputation had fallen and the painting's direct dependence on Castiglione's early pictures, in which large animals similarly fill the foreground. As was true for Castiglione and for every painter of such subjects in Genoa during the seventeenth century, the influence of Flemish masters working in Genoa, especially Jan Roos and Pieter Boel, was crucial. The most striking aspect of *Th Larder* is the sustained effort by the artist to evoke the corporeal presence of each separate object or animal. These qualities were shared by many Genoese and Spanish painters of the period, which might account for the attempts to identify the artist as a Spaniard.

1) Soprani, 1674, pp. 227-229.
2) O. Grosso, 1923, pp. 502ff.
3) P. Torriti, 1971, p. 335.
4) F. R. Shapley, 1979, p. 516.
5) Genoa, 1969, no. 69, repr.
6) A. Percy, 1971, p. 53 note 80.

5

The ample production of Felice Boselli has recently been examined in a monumental catalogue raisonné by Ferdinando Arisi (1973). No less than 514 paintings are attributed to Boselli therein, and additional still lifes from his hand continue to be discovered.

Born in Piacenza, the son of a shoemaker, Felice Boselli was apprenticed to Giuseppe Nuvolone in Milan, ca. 1665. He returned to Piacenza in 1669, seemingly because of his father's inability to pay his expenses. By 1673, the young artist was married, a father, and resident in Parma, the capital of the Farnese duchy. Except for periods spent in the service of various Farnese dependencies, Parma would be the center of his activity for the remainder of his long life.

Although Boselli is not known to have travelled beyond the Po valley, there was hardly a still life precedent that did not find expression on at least a few occasions in his encyclopedic development. He painted every sort of still life subject (except musical instruments), with frequent reminiscences of such artists as Vincenzo Campi, Pieter Boel, Jan Fyt, Michelangelo Cerquozzi, Giuseppe Maria Crespi, and Angelo Maria Crivelli. He may have been open to outside suggestion because of the lack of a coherent tradition of still life painting in his native Emilia. For the most part his art hearkens back to the late sixteenth-century pioneers of naturalism in North Central Italy: Vincenzo Campi in Cremona, Annibale Carracci and Bartolomeo Passarotti in Bologna. Boselli shared his forebears' appreciation for a broad, popular brand of humor.

The earliest dated painting by Boselli is a small still life of various birds, signed and dated 1680 (Bottari collection, Parma); its clarity of design is a passing reference to Evaristo Baschenis's still lifes of such subjects. From 1681-1690, Boselli was employed by Count Alessandro Sanvitale for fresco and tempera decorations in the theatre (destroyed ca. 1875) at Fontanellato, scene of famous festivals for which Boselli may have designed settings. He also painted portraits and still lifes for the Sanvitale castle at Fontanellato. For the Meli Lupi, nobles of Soragna, Boselli painted in 1698 a *Resurrected Christ* for the Oratorio di S. Croce, Soragna. The same patrons commissioned for their castle in 1699 Boselli's decorative masterpieces, a series of six oval compositions of still lifes, mostly of fish, accompanied by figures of children at play. A second series of six oval still lifes was commissioned by the Meli Lupi in 1708. His altarpiece of *Ecce Homo* in S. Brigida, Piacenza, dates from 1702. At some point before 1707, Boselli returned to Fontanellato to execute copies in twelve canvases (Parma, Galleria Nazionale) of the famous frescoes of *Diana and Actaeon* by Parmigianino. The latest documented works by the artist are a pair of still lifes in the Galleria Campori, Modena, with dates of March 4th and March 29th, 1730 on their versos and the inscription: "Felix Boselli completed this at age 79."

The contemporary reputation enjoyed by Boselli may be surmised from the inclusion of ten paintings by Boselli in an exhibition in Florence in 1737 [1].

36. A Butcher Shop

Oil on canvas. 134x174 cm.
Provenance: Avv. Maggi collection, Piacenza; Conte L. Zauli Naldi collection, Faenza, gift.
References: U. Ojetti, L. Dami and N. Tarchiani, 1922, p. 43 no. 147; G. De Logu, 1962, pp. 73, 177-178, pl. 37; Naples, Palazzo Reale, 1964, no 103; A. Ghidiglia Quintavalle, 1971, p. 236; F. Arisi, 1973, pp. 284-285, cat. no. 425.

Faenza, Pinacoteca Comunale.

In a curious incidence of historical symmetry, Felice Boselli took up the theme of the butcher shop at the turn of the eighteenth century, at the moment when the gathered energy that had propelled Italian still life painting through the transformations of Baroque style began perceptibly to disperse. The momentum had been set into motion, slightly more than a century before, by paintings of this same theme by Vincenzo Campi in Cremona, and Annibale Carracci and Bartolomeo Passarotti in Bologna (cf. R.F. 4). It was not by chance, perhaps, that Boselli knew in the Farnese

Fig. 29. Felice Boselli, Butcher Shop. *Museo Rizzi, Sestri Levante.*

collection in Parma the same paintings of this theme by Joachim
Beuckelaer that had so impressed Campi, Passarotti and Carracci.
In the interim between the paintings of the Carracci, for example,
and Felice Boselli, the striving for naturalism that these sixteenth
century artists had so boldly advanced had been achieved (at the
turn of the seventeenth century) but a process of compromise had
soon begun. By the date, ca. 1720, of Boselli's *Butcher Shop* there
was little point to querying after the artist's adherence to nature.
Notwithstanding the subject matter, Boselli's purpose in his still
lifes was to amuse the viewer with the slightly comic animation of
his design and the virtuoso freedom of his brushwork. It remains
an open question as to whether Boselli has emulated the
allegorical content of his sixteenth-century models or merely the
aspects of caricature [2].
Boselli occasionally repeated motifs from one picture to another.
Giuseppe De Logu was the first to observe that most of the
offerings of this butcher shop were painted again, with different
figures, in a *Butcher Shop* in the Museo Rizzi, Sestri Levante
(fig. 29) [3].

1) S. F. Borrani, 1974, p. 68.

2) In any context, and especially in the midst of so much flesh, the man's act of
weighing with a scale could very well be a Vanitas reference to the Day of
Judgment. This kind of subject matter would be quite unusual in Boselli's *oeuvre*.

3) G. De Logu, 1962, pp. 177-178. Cf. F. Arisi, 1973, nos. 426, 327, 183 for three
borrowings.

The style practiced by the highly successful Cristoforo Munari at the turn of the eighteenth century can be considered representative of the general situation of still life painting in Rome, Tuscany, and Emilia at that time. The circumstances of Munari's training are not known; his native Reggio Emilia could not have offered him much direction in the painting of still lifes. He presumably gravitated towards Bologna, as his first documented activity finds him in Rome in the service of Cardinal Imperiali, 1703, and acquainted with the Bolognese painter D. M. Muratori. Although Evaristo Baschenis has frequently been invoked as an influence on Munari, the occurence of Lombard subject matter in Munari's work was most likely inspired by the still lifes of Pier Francesco Cittadini, the transplanted Milanese, whose paintings could be seen in Bologna, Modena and Sassuolo. As Giuliano Briganti was the first to observe, however, it was in Rome in contact with the German still life painter Christian Berentz (1658-1722) that Munari's artistic personality received its strongest impulse [1]. Berentz was the leading exponent in Rome of a Dutch-influenced taste for still lifes of fine objects — crystal glasses, silver platters, Delftware — arranged in a kind of genteel disorder (none of the gaudy profusion of Fieravino, Il Maltese) and described in loving detail. As interpreted by Cristoforo Munari, who brought to it a capacity to compose on a large scale, this style was eminently suitable for the decoration of courtly interiors.

An exchange of letters between Munari in Rome (4 November 1705) and Prince Ferdinando de' Medici of Tuscany (5 January 1706) includes references to paintings sent to the duke of Modena and to Prince Ferdinando [2]. After his arrival in Florence in 1706, Munari painted many still lifes for the local nobility. Marrini (1764) describes in detail the *trompe l'oeil* compositions of Munari, many of which adorned the Villa di Lappeggi, the favorite retreat of Cardinal Francesco Maria de' Medici. This facet of the artist's *oeuvre* (which seems to have launched a *trompe l'oeil* craze in Tuscany) has been rediscovered only recently [3]. One of Munari's paintings was hung with the select pictures in the apartments of Prince Ferdinando in the Villa del Poggio a Caiano. According to Marrini, Munari was an able restorer of old paintings, for which purpose he was called in 1715 to work in the Duomo of Pisa.

37. Still Life with Musical Instruments

Oil on canvas. 99x134 cm.
Provenance: Medici collections; Villa Poggio a Caiano (Inv. 1890 no. 7591).
References: G. De Logu, 1955, fig. 5; G. De Logu, 1962, p. 178; A. Ghidiglia Quintavalle, 1964, cat. no. 3; M. Rosci, 1977, p. 241, pl. L.
Florence, Galleria degli Uffizi.

Except for the handling of the paint, which is more dense, and for the relative largeness of the individual forms, this *Still Life with Musical Instruments* by Cristoforo Munari could almost be taken for the work of a Dutch artist. Munari's preferred repertory of motifs (violin, violincello, flute, trombone and lute, peeled lemon, and even Delftware) were each of them the standard fare of the Dutch school before Munari was born. The tilted dish of fruit was almost the signature of Jan Davidsz de Heem, whose style was propagated in Italy with unnerving fidelity (coming from an Italian) by Andrea Benedetti, who actually studied with De Heem in Antwerp. Benedetti returned to Italy after 1649, the personification of the Italian enthusiasm for Northern European still lifes. Munari did not assimilate the Dutch modes to such an extreme degree, however. In his finest works, as in this one, he mitigated Northern linearity with his broader technique and his sensitivity to geometric shapes. His depiction of Delftware cups on their side or right-side up — to call attention to their outlines — occurs frequently enough to seem a signature.
A. Ghidiglia Quintavalle has proposed to date this *Still Life with Musical Instruments* to ca. 1709. A comparable still life by Munari, signed and dated in that year, is also in the Uffizi, with a Medici collections provenance (fig. 30).

1) G. Briganti, 1954 (2), pp. 40-42.

2) Documents discovered by Marco Chiarini; see Detroit, 1974, p. 290.

3) See A. Veca, 1980, nos. XXII-XXIII; also A. Ghidiglia Quintavalle, 1964, no. 4.

Fig. 30. *Cristoforo Munari,* Still Life with Musical Instruments. *Galleria degli Uffizi, Florence.*

Bartolomeo del Bimbo, called Il Bimbi
Settignano 1648 - 1730 Florence

The unusual career of Bartolomeo Bimbi is known to us in detail thanks to the biography compiled by Francesco Saverio Baldinucci, a friend of the artist [1]. The young Bimbi received a conventional training as a figure painter first with Lorenzo Lippi in Florence, then in the studio of Onorio Marinari, after the death of Lippi in 1665. Bimbi travelled to Rome in the entourage of Cardinal Leopoldo de' Medici for the conclave of 1670 in which Pope Clement X was elected. In Rome for most of the year, the artist was employed by Pietro Susinni in the painting of copies, especially of portraits. He made the acquaintance of Mario dei Fiori, the famed painter of flower pictures, but showed as yet no interest in still lifes.

Upon his return to Florence, Bimbi re-entered the workshop of Marinari, and occupied himself with copies after other masters, as well as architectural decorations, grotesques, in various Florentine houses. Baldinucci reports that Bimbi's copies after the paintings of Carlo Dolci were especially fine and many of them were sold to foreign visitors.

After these mediocre beginnings, the career of Bimbi reached a turning point. Inspired one day by a large painting of a garland of flowers that he had seen in the studio of Agnolo Gori, Bimbi returned home and tried his hand at the same subject. His picture was admired by Prete Filizio Pizzichi, who introduced the artist to Grand Prince Ferdinando de' Medici. Prince Ferdinando acquired his first attempt at still life and began the practice of sending to Bimbi the rarest and most beautiful flowers, which the artist would immediately depict on canvas. As a painter of flowers, Bimbi evidently enjoyed a grand success with the Medici court and the Florentine nobility to judge from the copious citations of his flower pieces in eighteenth-century exhibitions in Florence. Most of his work in this genre remains to be rediscovered. In 1692 in collaboration with Anton Domenico Gabbiani (figures) and Pandolfo Reschi (landscapes), Bimbi decorated the mirrors in the Galleria of the Palazzo Medici-Riccardi.

The most noted aspect of Bartolomeo Bimbi's activity, and the light in which he is represented in this exhibition, was his service for Grand Duke Cosimo III and Prince Ferdinando de' Medici as the semi-official portraitist of botannical and zoological varieties and monstrosities. The Medici court, it may be remembered, initiated still life painting in Florence during the late sixteenth century with the employment of Jacopo Ligozzi as illustrator of natural science specimens. The scope of Bartolomeo Bimbi's subject matter was expanded to encompass not only every sort of fig, cherry, pear, apple, lemon, and so on from the famous Medici gardens, but also every sort known to exist. Florentine science was keen on oddities, and Bimbi was entrusted to record for posterity giant pumpkins, cauliflowers, radishes and truffles, a ferocious wolf that menaced the Mugello one year, not to mention the flock of birds that was precipitated by a sudden frost in 1718 in the marshes of Pisa. Most of Bimbi's paintings in this genre bear explanatory inscriptions; dated examples are known from the period 1696-1719.

From the accounts of Baldinucci and other eye-witnesses, we learn that Grand Duke Cosimo III filled La Topaia, his *casino*, or summer house above the Villa of Castello, with Bimbi's paintings of fruits and flowers. The Medici Villa dell'Imbrogiana was famous for its decoration with paintings of fish and wild-life by Bimbi and other artists. The dimensions (and character) of these collections seem to have had a boggling effect on visitors. " Anton Domenico Gabbiani, having seen and considered the decoration of La Topaia, said, stupified (*pieno di stupore*) to the Grand Duke himself that neither Titian nor Raphael nor any painter of the world who had wished to paint fruits and flowers, could ever have made them in such an imaginative form and so well. " [2] Baldinucci reports that no admirer of painting when visiting Florence failed to make his way to Castello and La Topaia.

38. Citrons and Lemons
Oil on canvas. 176x230 cm.
Provenance: Medici Collections, Villa di Castello (Inv. 597)
Reference: S. Meloni Trkulja, 1968, p. 460.
Florence, Palazzo Pitti, Galleria Palatina.

Fig. 31. Bartolomeo Bimbi, Lemons and Citrons. *Galleria Palatina, Palazzo Pitti, Florence.*

At the end of the seventeenth century, Cosimo III, Grand Duke of Tuscany, called upon the talents of Bartolomeo Bimbi to provide a new form of still life decoration for the *casino*, La Topaia, at the Villa di Castello. The decoration of countryside villas with still life paintings or frescoed programs of the Four Seasons, the Four Elements, and other allusions to agriculture was, of course, traditional. It was the unprecedented conception of Cosimo III, inspired by the scientific aspirations of his time, to decorate La Topaia as a kind of gallery of botannical reference and natural science curiosities. Appropriate specimens were sent to Bimbi to be painted, forming a collection that was acclaimed in its day. With time and the dispersal of the furnishings of La Topaia the paintings by Bimbi were forgotten. In 1960, Giuseppe De Logu was the first to identify several grand paintings of cherries, figs, and other fruits in storage at the Palazzo Pitti with the dismantled decorations of La Topaia [3]. The over-sized *Lemons and Citrons* in this exhibition and a pendant canvas with still more *Lemons and Citrons* (Inv. Castello 616) (fig. 31) were likewise painted by Bimbi for La Topaia and are the most recent rediscoveries of the group [4].

As more and more paintings from La Topaia have been identified, it has become possible to imagine the scope and extravagance of the original setting. Although Bimbi has been criticized by some modern scholars for his " self-effacement " in his illustrational role, the artist's contemporary biographer, F. S. Baldinucci, informs us that the imagination and beauty of the artist's depictions of fruits and vegetables were universally praised. Even while meeting the condition of precise description, Bimbi was able to invent a variety of contexts for his subjects: the cherries spill out of a basket, the figs are piled in heaps on platters. These lemons are arrayed on a leafy arbor, of which the lattice work can be seen at the top. Two herms, typical garden sculptures, stand at either side. Unlike the other paintings for La Topaia, this *Lemons and Citrons* clearly displays its function as large-scale wall ornament. The paintings of cherries, figs, and pears which are currently on view at the Palazzo Pitti, make use of compositional formats similar to those that had been developed by Pier Francesco Cittadini in Bologna. There are no antecedents in the tradition of still life painting for Bimbi's arbors of lemons and citrons. They were invented to fulfill a specific purpose at La Topaia as parts of an energetic and slightly bizarre decorative plan.

1) The biography of Bimbi remained in manuscript until 1975: F. S. Baldinucci (A. Matteoli, ed.), Rome, 1975, pp. 239-253.

2) *Ibid.*, p. 249.

3) G. De Logu, 1960, pp. 59-66, was unaware of the biography by F. S. Baldinucci, and could only point to general references to Bimbi's still lifes at the Villa di Castello.

4) I am grateful to Marco Chiarini for bringing these paintings to my attention.

Some notable still lifes of fruit have been ascribed to Giovanni
Paolo Spadino, but biographical details remain scarce. The artist's
presence in Florence and his profession as a still life painter are
documented by his signed receipt of July 14, 1687 of payment
from marchese Filippo Corsini for two paintings of fruit [1]. In June
of 1689, Cardinal Flavio I Chigi received in Rome a "painting of
fruit, of an apple, which came from Florence, made by Spadino." [2]
The simple signature *Spadino* is known from three signed and
dated still lifes: the earliest (Roccamadoro Ramelli collection,
Fermo) is inscribed, *Roma 1701*; the two other signed works
(Galleria Capitolina, Rome (fig. 32) and formerly Nigro collection
Genoa) are both inscribed *Roma 1703* [3]. These signed pictures are
quite consistent in style and have been the touchstones for
additional attributions, of which the most important picture is a
large *Still Life with Parrot* in the Museo Fesch, Ajaccio (R.P. 48).
Notwithstanding the artist's early residence in Florence, the
paintings in the Spadino *corpus* are linked by their Roman
qualities and late Baroque style. There are references both to
Michelangelo da Campidoglio (as in the Ajaccio picture) and to
the contemporary works of Christian Berentz. Spadino displays a
playful spirit which often appears in his predilection for coiled
loops of vines and over-sized white highlights.
A Neapolitan sojourn by Spadino may be indicated by the
presence of eight small still lifes attributed to "Spatini" in the
1715 inventory of the collection of Principe Giacomo Capece
Zurlo, Naples [4]. The Capace Zurlo collection was comprised
almost exclusively of paintings by Neapolitan masters or of artists
who worked in Naples.
In 1968, the process of reconstruction of the *oeuvre* of Giovanni
Paolo Spadino was rendered provisional by a suggestion by
Ferdinando Bologna that the paintings signed *Spadino* as well as
others by the same hand were in fact the work of a certain
Bartolomeo Spadino [5]. Prof. Bologna reported the existence in
Rome of a signed example by Bartolomeo that was comparable to
the paintings previously believed by Giovanni Paolo. In the
Enciclopedia (1817-24) of Pietro Zani, a Bartolomeo Spadino
and a Giovanni Paolo Spadino are both named, without however,
any other information [6]. For Giovanni Paolo Spadino, F. Bologna
has proposed a newly found group of still lifes of more restrained
composition, one of which is inscribed *Spadino*. The proposals
advanced by F. Bologna must be considered hypotheses pending
the publication of the paintings on which his argument is based,
especially those bearing the name of the elusive Bartolomeo
Spadino.

39. Still Life with Melons
Oil on canvas. 79.5x152 cm.
Unpublished.
New York, Private Collection.

This imposing *Still Life with Melons* was previously attributed to
Michelangelo Pace, called Michelangelo da Campidoglio, who
was the leading native proponent of Roman High Baroque still life
painting (cf. R.P. 34-35). Roman qualities are indeed foremost in
this painting: the grandeur and weightiness that the artist has seen
in these simple fruits are characteristic of the Roman vision of art.
The arrangement of the fruit in rows on a table-top recalls the
earliest tradition of still life painting in the Eternal City.
Certain other qualities dictate a date later than the span of
Campidoglio's career (pre-1670) and are otherwise unlike his
style. Campidoglio's still lifes are distinguished by the dynamic
High Baroque sense of continuity between foreground and
distance. The artist of this *Still Life with Melons* evinces the
concerns of a younger generation in that spatial recession is
minimized in favor of an energetic pattern which fills the picture
surface. Nor does this younger generation share Campidoglio's
interest in sensuous textures; the surface of this *Still Life with
Melons* is unified by its consistency of handling: the white
highlights that enliven the composition appear the same whether
applied to the figs, or to the pears, for example.

Fig. 32. Giovanni Paolo Spadino, Still Life with Melon. *Galleria Capitolina.
Rome.*

9

In the opinion of this writer, the technique employed in this *Still Life with Melons* is sufficiently comparable to that of the *Still Life* in the Galleria Capitolina, Rome (fig. 32) by Giovanni Paolo Spadino to justify the attribution of the picture to the latter's authorship. The most striking coincidences pertain to the brushwork and the palette, difficult aspects to compare in photographs. In both pictures, the melons are painted with short, dense strokes which give relief to the canvas. In most of the paintings with persuasive attributions to Spadino, the artist's free use of white highlights and curling vines becomes close to a mannerism; these elements are present in this *Still Life* in only a nascent stage — which is to say that the painting appears to be earlier in date than the works thus far attributed to G. P. Spadino. There is in any event a monumentality in these forms which pertains to the grander style of the seventeenth century, and not to the lighter decorations of the eighteenth century.

In the right-hand corner of this canvas at the bottom there appears a prominent inventory number (305), which, when identified, should help to establish the history of this painting.

1) See G. De Logu, 1962, p. 186.

2) See *Ibid.*, p. 186.

3) The painting in the Nigro collection appeared with an unsigned pendent on the art market in Milan in 1965 (Finarte 19, 24 November 1965, lots 36a and 36b).

4) R. Ruotolo, 1973, p. 149: "Otto quadretti di frutti Spatini, misura 2 e 1 1/2, cornice di pero, d. 80."

5) F. Bologna, 1968, no. 48.

6) Cited by *Ibid.*, no. 48.

he Abate Andrea Belvedere, with whom the great age of
eapolitan still life painting closed, was moreover a leading
ntributor to the theatre and literary world of Naples. His early
aining as an artist is unclear. He could not have studied with
olo Porpora, who had relocated to Rome by 1654, nor does his
rly style reflect any direct influence of Giovan Battista
uoppolo; these masters were the two possibilities raised by B. De
ominici (1742).
he whole course of Belvedere's career as a painter was contained
ithin the seventeenth century. Although De Dominici mentions
ll lifes of fruits, flowers and birds — and two fish still lifes by
m are known — Belvedere was first and last a specialist in
ower-pieces. His activity begins in the early 1670's with vases of
owers painted in strict emulation of the earliest still lifes of the
eapolitan school — the simple, severe flower paintings of
iacomo Recco.
ter the arrival of Abraham Brueghel in Naples in 1675, the
ecorative winds that had drifted down from the Roman school
ere now present in gale force. Belvedere's response to the
erated compositions of Brueghel and of Franz Werner von
amm (whom De Dominici singles out as an influence [1]; Tamm
as in Rome ca. 1685-1695) was to expand his vision just enough
take in the secluded corner of a garden, for example, with
owers and their reflections in a pool seen with the vividness of a
eam. He also collaborated in the Roman fashion with Francesco
olimena, painting flowers to Solimena's *putti* [2].
1694 (ca.), Andrea Belvedere was called to the court of Spain
Carlo II, apparently on the suggestion of Luca Giordano. His
ower-pieces during this period declined to expert, but empty
itations of the style of Mario dei Fiori (R.P. 8-9). De Dominici
ates that Belvedere returned to Naples after Luca Giordano had
nbarrassed him in front of the Spanish court; however, his
turn in 1700 may merely have been occasioned by the death of
arlos II.
pon his return to Naples, Belvedere ceased to paint in order to
vote himself to the comic theatre: he was the principal adaptor
d arranger for the Neapolitan stage of Spanish
sword-and-cape" comedies. Raffaello Causa has commented
at Belvedere may have abandoned the field of art because after
700 the Neapolitan school was bereft of worthy colleagues [3].

40. Carnations in a Vase
Oil on canvas. 100x41 cm.
Provenance: Museo Duca di Martina, Naples.
References: R. Causa, *Andrea Belvedere, pittore di fiori*, Milan,
1964; R. Causa, 1972, p. 1023; M. Rosci, 1977, pp. 110, 176.
Naples, Museo Nazionale di Capodimonte.

41. Tulips in a Vase
Oil on canvas. 99.5x41 cm.
Provenance: Museo Duca di Martina, Naples.
References: R. Causa, *Andrea Belvedere, pittore di fiori*, Milan,
1964; R. Causa, 1972, p. 1023; M. Rosci, 1977, pp. 110, 176.
Naples, Museo Nazionale di Capodimonte.

This pair of flower still lifes is representative of the severe,
purposefully archaic style of Andrea Belvedere's first decade of
activity. The painstaking naturalism and the sober expression of
the young artist's initial style of the 1570's was an unexpected
development of direct opposition to the decorative conceptions of
still life that had already become predominant by this time. Only
in certain works by Giuseppe Recco can comparable expressions
of restraint be found. Belvedere's sensitivity for poignant
understatement anticipated the most valuable developments in
eighteenth-century European, not only Neapolitan, still life
painting, as R. Causa has perceptively observed [4].
The artist painted this same combination of flowers, viewed
singly, in another pair of canvases in the Museo Correale,
Sorrento: *Carnations in a Glass Vase* and *Tulips in a Glass Vase* [5].
The conjunction of tulips and carnations has symbolic overtones
appropriate to the dignity of Belvedere's conceptions. Both
flowers were particular attributes of the Virgin Mary and were
emblematic of Divine Love [6]. This inclusion of allegorical content
was another act by Belvedere of resistance against prevailing
tendencies.

1) R. Causa, 1972, p. 1024, clarifies this confusing passage in B. De Dominici,
1742, III, p. 571.
2) B. De Dominici, *op. cit.*, p. 571; See Madrid, 1970, no. 12.
3) R. Causa, 1972, p. 1025.
4) *Ibid.*, p. 1023.
5) See Naples, Palazzo Reale, 1964, nos. 107 and 108, repr.
6) M. L. D'Ancona, 1977, pp. 79-80 (red carnations), 390 (tulip).

e documentation concerning Giacomo Nani is not extensive,
t a good many signed still lifes by him are known. None of his
ntings are dated. Nani was born in Porto Ercole, a Spanish
pendency near Grosseto. In 1739 a Neapolitan document refers
his arrival in Naples 28 years before, that is, ca. 1711, at the age
hirteen [1].
De Dominici (1742) states that Giacomo Nani was a pupil of
spare Lopez, a flower specialist. From Lopez, Nani adopted a
de, imitative of Andrea Belvedere, of diminutive landscapes or
dens with statuary strewn with tiny flowers. The still life
ntings of game and birds by Baldassare De Caro and the
mble kitchen still lifes (cucine povere) by Tommaso Realfonzo,
th followers of Belvedere, likewise were determinant influences
Giacomo Nani. An aspect of his career which remains to be
estigated is his service (documented 1754) for Carlos III as a
signer and painter at the Royal Porcelain Factory at
podimonte [2].
any paintings by Nani were sent to Spain; it has been suggested,
reover, that Nani's style was influential on Luis Meléndez, the
nous Spanish still life painter who was born in Naples in 1716 [3].
riano Nani (ca. 1725-1804), the son of Giacomo, left Naples
Madrid in 1759, where he painted still lifes that are
mparable to the style of Meléndez [4].

42. Still Life with Prosciutto and Birds

Oil on canvas. 65x78 cm.
Signed: *Giacomo Nani f.*
References: G. De Logu, 1962, p. 199, pl. 101; Naples, Palazzo
Reale, 1964, no. 123; M. Rosci, 1977, p. 205.
Naples, Museo Nazionale della Certosa di S. Martino.

This *Still Life with Prosciutto and Birds*, like much of Giacomo
Nani's *oeuvre*, looks back to seventeenth-century models, as by
Giovan Battista Ruoppolo or Giovanni Battista Recco, but
presents them in a minor key, so to speak. The physical presences
of the still life elements are not the concern of Nani so much as the
achievement of a pervasive tonality. Although a painter of
decorations, pure and simple, Nani possesses an unexpectedly
blunt vision of reality which often leads to awkward results. In his
finest paintings, of which this *Still Life with Prosciutto and Birds* is
certainly one, Nani's simple draftsmanship and moderated tones
strike a balance that just allows the name of one of the artist's
contemporaries to be mentioned in a whisper: *Chardin*.

1) U. Prota-Giurleo, 1953, p. 57.
2) See Naples, 1979/80, II, p. 121.
3) R. Causa, 1972, p. 1055.
4) See Madrid, 1979/80, no. 119.

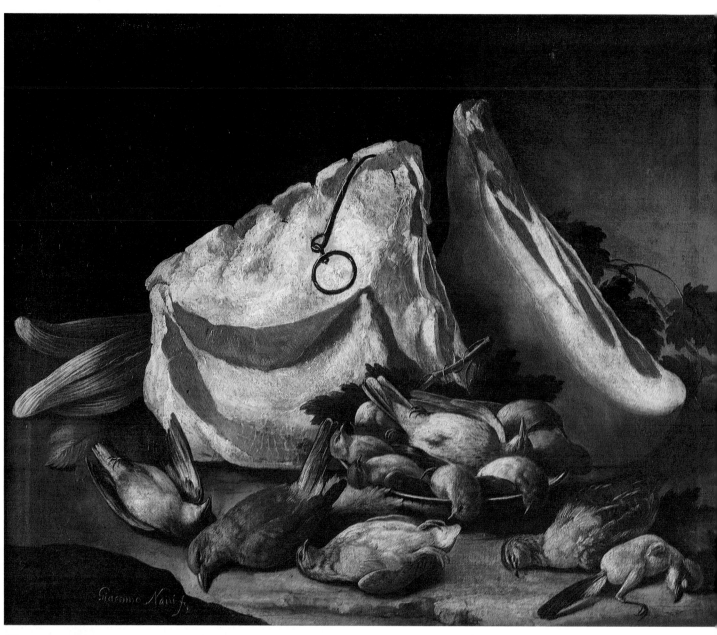

ne name of the artist appears variously as Niccolino anhoubracken, Niccolò Vanderbrach; Van Bubrachen, 'an-oubru-Ken, Valdubrochen and Niccola Messinese. An aportant master of still life subjects in Tuscany during the early ghteenth century, Van Houbraken was rediscovered by G. J. oogewerff (1930), who identified a painting executed by the tist for Antonio Della Seta of Pisa in 1704. Other valuable tices concerning the artist were introduced by M. Gregori in the talogue of the "Natura Morta Italiana" exhibition in Naples in 064.

an Houbraken was born in Messina, Sicily, into a family of emish painters. In 1674 his family relocated in Livorno on the aiscan coast. From Livorno, Van Houbraken sent paintings of lowers, fruits, plants and animals" to "various places, his orks being appreciated by everyone" (P. A. Orlandi, 1719). everal paintings of fruit and flowers by Van Houbraken were cluded in the 1706 and 1729 exhibitions of S. Luca in the oister of SS. Annunziata, Florence [1]. A landscape by the artist ith figures by another hand was also exhibited in 1706 [2]. M. regori was able to identify a reference to a portrait of Francesco ivière by Van Houbraken in the exhibition of 1729 with a ainting in the Galleria degli Uffizi, traditionally considered a lf-portrait of Van Houbraken [3]. Another notable addition to the cure oeuvre of the artist was recently made by M. Chiarini, who entified an unattributed Still Life in the Palazzo Pitti with a escription of a picture by "Niccola Messinese" in the 1713 ventory of the collection of Grand Prince Ferdinando de' edici [4].

ne collection of drawings made by cav. F. M. Gaburri of Florence cluded a drawing by "Nicola Wan Oubrachen". The sheet is escribed by Gaburri himself in the 1722 catalogue of his ollection along with the note that Van Houbraken, "a Fleming ving in Livorno, made the drawing expressly for him [Gaburri] in 718" [5].

43. Still Life with Wine Bottles and Oysters
Oil on canvas. 120.7x163.8 cm.
Provenance: David M. Koetser, gift.
Unpublished.
Los Angeles, Los Angeles County Museum of Art.

The present attribution of this Still Life with Wine Bottles and Oysters derives from the close resemblance of this painting to a Still Life in the Palazzo Pitti, Florence (fig. 33), which was added to the oeuvre of Nicola Van Houbraken by M. Gregori in 1964 [6]. The attribution of the Palazzo Pitti Still Life to Van Houbraken was based on its relationship to the picture that had earlier been documented by the research of G. J. Hoogewerff (1930); subsequent research has confirmed the common authorship of the paintings assigned to the artist.
It is possible, in fact, that the Still Life with Wine Bottles and Oysters from Los Angeles was painted as a pendant to the Palazzo Pitti Still Life. The dimensions of the picture in Florence, 115x160 cm., are essentially the same. The two paintings have several motifs in common and are similarly composed; in each, the clutter of still life is contrasted against the broad surface of the background wall. In addition, both of these still lifes were painted from a low point of view, evidently so that they could serve as overdoor decorations [7].
The assembled works of Nicola Van Houbraken reveal him as an artist of Northern extraction who has fully assimilated into the Italian school. The only overt passages of Flemish technique in his paintings are the dry, sometimes silky textures imparted to leaves, stalks of celery, and the like. The artist's preferred harmonies of warm tones of green and brown are reminiscent of eighteenth-century Lombard colors, although the explanation for this coincidence is not known [8].

Fig. 33. Nicola Van Houbraken, Still Life. Galleria Palatina, Palazzo Pitti, Florence.

1) *Nota de' Quadri* etc., 1706; *Nota de' Quadri e Opere di Scultura* etc., 1729.

2) *Nota de' Quadri* etc., 1706, p. 18: "Un Paese di Van hubrachen, con Figure del Genovese" [figures by Magnasco?], without indication of collection.

3) M. Gregori in Naples, Palazzo Reale, 1964, no. 185.

4) M. Chiarini, 1975, pp. 81, 104 note 219, fig. 69a.

5) G. Campori, 1870, pp. 569-70, no. 468.

6) M. Gregori, *op. cit.*, no. 186. Palazzo Pitti inv. 1890 n. 5136; G. De Logu, 1962, pp. 97-98, had previously commented on the Italian/Flemish character of this painting. A second *Still Life* in the Palazzo Pitti (inv. 1890 n. 5137) with the same dimensions, 118x156 cm., was attributed by G. De Logu to the same anonymous hand, and considered by M. Gregori to be a pendant by Van Houbraken.

7) Scott Shaeffer, who kindly brought the LACM *Still Life* to my attention, first suggested that this "Italian school" picture might have been made as an overdoor.

8) A pair of still lifes of wine bottles and onions — by Van Houbraken, in the opinion of this writer — are attributed in a London private collection to Giacomo Ceruti. Mention may be made here of a pair of untraced still lifes of various plants, violets, and a horse skull, ascribed to "Valdubrochen" in the 1752 inventory of Vincenzo Riccardi, Florence; see G. de Juliis, 1981, p. 69 no. 54.

During the first half of the eighteenth century, Faenza, Ravenna and other cities in the province of Romagna were graced by the career of the Abate Arcangelo Resani, whose talents were not provincial. According to P. A. Orlandi (1719), who may have been acquainted with the artist, Resani was born in Rome of a Genoese father. He studied painting in Rome with G. B. Buoncuore, a pupil of P. F. Mola and follower of Guercino. Given these influences, it is not surprising that Resani transferred to Bologna at the age of nineteen to begin his career.

His speciality from the first was the depiction of animals. G. P. Zanotti (1739) noted that his abilities were appreciated and made use of by the leading artists of the Bolognese school, Pasinelli and Dal Sole among them. Within a brief time, however, Resani took up residence in Forlì. During this early period, the artist is reported by P. A. Orlandi to have worked in Siena, Venice, and also different cities in Romagna. From various sources it appears that Faenza and Ravenna (documented 1736) were the centers of his mature activity.

A painting of *Mercury and Argus* (Vienna, Dorotheum, 29 November 1977, lot 104), signed and dated 1705, is the earliest work by Resani that has appeared. He was a capable painter of the human figure as well and seems often to have painted figurative subjects (after the Genoese and Flemish practice) that called for the conspicuous presence of animals. There also exist early references to altarpieces executed by him in Forlì and Ravenna, and even a cupola in Faenza. A *Goatherd and his Flock* (Muratori collection, Ferrara) is signed and dated 1713. In August of 1713, Resani's *Self-Portrait* (fig. 34) entered the Uffizi collection of Cosimo III of Tuscany. Another *Self-Portrait* inscribed (by another hand) *Arcangelus Resani Romanus pictor celeberrimus pinxit se ipsum anno 1724 aetatis suae 54* was formerly in the Homme collection, Vienna[1]. The artist was elected an honorary Academician of the Accademia Clementina in Bologna in 1722, an honor for which he was doubly qualified since he was also a respected poet.

Despite the number of paintings (almost invariably of animals) that are ascribed to Resani in old inventories, for the moment, his works are unaccountably rare. Less than twenty paintings by him have been identified to date.

44. Dog and Basket
Oil on canvas. 58x73 cm.
Provenance: Bosi collection (1931).
References: G. Bargellesi, 1961, p. 156; G. De Logu, 1962, p. 176; Naples, Palazzo Reale, 1964, no. 283; E. Golfieri, *Pinacoteca di Faenza*, Faenza, 1964, no. 26; A. Corbara, 1965, p. 54; E. Riccomini, 1974, p. 63; M. Rosci, 1977, p. 210; F. Bologna, 1979, no. 333.
Faenza, Pinacoteca Comunale.

The summary title of this painting of a *Dog and Basket* scarcely does justice to the poetic resonance of this work. The authorship of Arcangelo Resani was only recognized in 1961 by G. Bargelles in the first reconsideration of the artist in modern times. Since th publication, the *Dog and Basket* has been by far the most admire picture among the artist's consistently excellent production.
The passwords in the artistic vocabulary of Resani are clarity and stillness. His paintings reveal an arcadian sensibility in the sense that their rustic subjects bespeak the artist's indomitable faith th the beauty and mystery of nature on any level cannot be equalled by art. In this *Dog and Basket*, as for instance in Resani's single

Fig. 34. Arcangelo Resani, Self-Portrait. *Galleria degli Uffizi, Florence.*

views of fallen birds, the presence of the painter between the viewer and the image is not felt. As an artist of the eighteenth century, Resani does not compose his subjects so that they project forward from the picture, as Baroque artists did, but he tightly encloses his still lifes within the picture frame to attain a concentration rarely found in the works of his contemporaries. In purely formal terms, the *Dog and Basket* appeals for the " singular modernity ", to quote R. Roli (1964), of the white and brown passage of painting that describes the form of the sleeping dog. The sources for Resani's style have not been determined. The Flemish painter of animals, Jan Fyt, has been mentioned but the similarity does not extend beyond the subject matter. Attempts to relate Resani to Bolognese tradition (which is not a cohesive entity, in any event) have not as yet been persuasive [2]. For this writer, the closest parallels are to be found in the " Spanish " quietude of certain Genoese still life paintings, as by G. A. Cassana, for example. Resani's still lifes are distinguished, of course, in this comparison by his Roman sensibility for dramatic compression.

1) See Bologna, 1979, under no. 332.
2) *Ibid.*, no. 33.

Three examples of the copious *oeuvre* of Carlo Magini were exhibited in the monumental exhibition of Italian painting at the Palazzo Pitti, Florence, in 1922 with attributions to an early seventeenth-century master [1]. In 1953, Roberto Longhi, and in 1954, Count Luigi Zauli Naldi published still lifes by Magini bearing his signature and the inscription (in French) " painter of Fano. " Subsequent researches have determined that Carlo Magini passed the entirety of his career in Fano (in the Marches) painting still lifes with an extraordinary constancy of vision. He also practised portraiture, in which field he was merely competent [2]. The artistic training of Magini is not known and could not have been extensive in his native town. However, his still life compositions are constructed with a sophistication and a technical mastery that belie the tag of " provincial artist " that is sometimes applied to him.

45. Kitchen Still Life
Oil on canvas. 59x78 cm.
Unpublished
Campione d'Italia, Silvano Lodi Collection.

46. Kitchen Still Life
Oil on canvas. 59x78 cm.
Unpublished
Campione d'Italia, Silvano Lodi Collection.

The scholarly euphoria with which newly discovered still life paintings by Carlo Magini were published during the 1950's has noticeably abated with the realization that Magini's still lifes mostly look alike. Rather than a cause for disappointment, however, this phenomenon is the source of their charm, evidently as the artist intended. Except for a few compositions of upright format, the preponderant majority of paintings by Magini are closely comparable to the two *Kitchen Still Lifes* in this exhibition. The motifs in Magini's still lifes have the familiarity of old friends: perhaps the green bottle stopped with a piece of paper is the most faithful member of the company, but there probably does not exist a still life by Magini that has not at least one motif in common with the pair here exhibited.
Charles Sterling has suggested that Magini descends from the naturalistic vision of Evaristo Baschenis [3]. Yet, a wide span of time divides the two. In the opinion of this writer, Magini's paintings can be related to the Florentine tradition of verisimilitude unto the point of *trompe l'oeil* that was inaugurated by Cristoforo Munari early in the eighteenth century. The still lifes by the under-documented Antonio Cioci, who was active in Florence contemporaneously with Magini, display the same tendency towards scattered arrangements of carefully defined objects. Although Magini's compositions are not *trompe l'oeil* deceptions, they are related to such by three considerations. In optical deceptions on the order of *trompe d'oeil*, the field of vision is necessarily restricted to within the reach of the viewer's hand, a condition observed by Magini. The potential of touch is essential to *trompe l'oeil* illusionism [4]. Secondly, Magini's repetition of a limited repertory of motifs is at the center of an optical witticism he plays, one that is analogous to *trompe l'oeil* in its manipulation of elements of time and space. A good part of the charm of any given still life by Magini is (for the initiated) the recognition of familiar motifs in new positions. The high frequency of pairs of still lifes in the artist's *oeuvre* is no accident, since the proximity of two examples naturally enhances this effect. When one looks from one of these *Kitchen Still Lifes* to the other, there arises the curious sense that the pestle has moments before shifted from one side of the mortar to the other, for example, or that the white jar is playing cat-and-mouse with the green bottle. Analogous incongruities lie behind the attraction of *trompe l'oeil*. Thirdly, Magini's still lifes and contemporary *trompe l'oeil* canvases share an aesthetic outlook in that both assume the viewer's readiness to accept a resolutely neutral description of reality. It is significant that Magini was active at the close of the last century prior to the invention of photography in 1839. Heinrich Schwarz has observed that Bernardo Bellotto (1720-1780) and other landscape painters of his generation [and of Magini's] pursued in

45

their paintings an absolute clarity which was finally achieved in photography [5]. Magini's aspirations in the field of still life were similarly in the forefront of late eighteenth-century painting.

1) As Paolo Antonio Barbieri. See G. De Logu, 1962, pp. 80-81, 179, for an account of the rediscovery of Magini.
2) See R. Roli, 1966, for illustrations.
3) C. Sterling, 2nd. rev. ed. 1981, p. 114.
4) See the essay by A. Veca, 1980, pp. 93-125, for a recent analysis of *trompe l'oeil*.
5) H. Schwarz, 1977, pp. 32 and 38.

1. *Carlo Crivelli,* Madonna and Child. *35x23 cm. ca. 1473. Metropolitan Museum of Art, New York.*

2. *Pieter Aertsen,* Kitchen Scene. *85x128 cm. 1562. National Museum, Stockholm.*

3. *Giovanni Battista Crespi, Il Cerano (attributed to),* Fruit Vendors, *1601. Wadsworth Atheneum, Hartford.*

4. *Bartolomeo Passarotti,* Butcher Shop, *112x152 cm. Palazzo Barberini, Rome.*

5. *Jacopo Ligozzi,* Mandrake Plant, *678x461 mm. Gabinetto Disegni e Stampe degli Uffizi, Florence.*

6. *Jan Brueghel de Velours (figures by Giulio Cesare Procaccini),* Garland of Flowers, *48x36 cm. Museo del Prado, Madrid.*

7. *Paolo Antonio Barbieri,* The Dispensary, *124x174 cm. Pinacoteca Civica, Spoleto.*

8. *Andrea Belvedere,* Vase of Flowers, *151x100 cm., signed AB. Museo del Prado, Madrid.*

9. *Andrea Belvedere,* Vase of Flowers, *151x100 cm., signed AB. Museo del Prado, Madrid.*

1

4

7

2

5

8

3

6

9

Bartolomeo Bettera, Still Life with Musical
[In]struments, *72x95 cm., signed* Bartolomeo Bettera
Accademia Carrara, Bergamo.

Bartolomeo Bettera, Still Life with Musical
[In]struments, *72x95 cm., signed* Bartolomeo Bettera
Accademia Carrara, Bergamo.

Bartolomeo Bimbi, Figs, *116x155 cm., signed*
[an]d dated B. B. 1696. *Galleria Palatina, Palazzo*
[Pit]ti, *Florence.*

13. *Pietro Paolo Bonzi, called Il Gobbo de' Carracci,*
Still Life, *100x136 cm, signed* P. Paolo di Cortona.
Lorenzelli Collection, Bergamo.

14. *Pietro Paolo Bonzi, called Il Gobbo de' Carracci
(attributed to),* Still Life with Fantastic Vase, *86x120
cm. Location unknown.*

15. *Felice Boselli,* Still Life with Chickens in a Pot.
Molinari Pradelli Collection, Bologna.

16. *Abraham Brueghel,* Flowers in a Sculpted Vase,
with Putti, *(figures by Guglielmo Cortese?),
120.6x203.2 cm., signed* A. Brughel F. *Formerly
Christie's, London, July 9, 1982, no. 14.*

17. *Margherita Caffi,* Vase of Flowers, *75x103 cm.,
signed* Marg. Caf. F. *Academia de San Fernando,
Madrid.*

18. *Margherita Caffi,* Vase of Flowers, *74x103 cm.,
signed* Marg. Caf. F. *Academia de San Fernando,
Madrid.*

10

13

16

11

14

17

12

15

18

19. *Giacomo da Castello*, Self-Portrait, *98.5x82.5 cm. Galleria degli Uffizi, Florence.*

20. *Michelangelo Cerquozzi*, Cincinnatus Called from Retirement, *ca. 200x300 cm., signed* MC *(in the vines). Private Collection.*

21. *Gaetano Cusati*, Still Life with Fish, *104x127 cm., signed* G. Cusati F. *Milwaukee Art Center.*

22. *Baldassare De Caro*, Still Life with Game, *126x101.5 cm., signed* B. De Caro. *Slive Collection, Cambridge, Mass.*

23. *Giacomo Fardella*, Still Life with Pigeons and Fruit. *Galleria Palatina, Palazzo Pitti (inv. 1890, 7578), Florence.*

24. *Francesco Fieravino, called Il Maltese*, Allegory of America, *78x112 cm. Menil Foundation, Houston.*

25. *Francesco Fieravino, called Il Maltese*, Still Life *Molinari Pradelli Collection, Bologna.*

26. *Luca Forte*, Vase of Flowers, *80x52 cm. Private Collection, London.*

27. *Luca Forte*, Vase of Flowers, *80x52 cm. Private Collection, London.*

28. *Onofrio Loth,* Still Life with Fish, *73x125 cm., signed Loth. f. Museo, Valencia.*

29. *Antonio Mara, called Il Scarpetta,* A Trompe Oeil Still Life, *58.5x73 cm., signed AMF, formerly Sotheby's, London, July 7, 1982. no. 308.*

30. *"The Master of Palazzo San Gervasio",* Still Life with a Bird in Flight, *170x245 cm. Pinacoteca Civica, Palazzo San Gervasio. Matera.*

31. *Mario Nuzzi, called Mario dei Fiori (figure by G. M. Morandi),* Portrait of Mario dei Fiori at his Easel, *195x265 cm. Chigi Collection, Ariccia.*

32. *Mario Nuzzi, called Mario dei Fiori,* A Vase of Flowers and a Basket of Flowers, *83x154 cm. Museo del Prado, Madrid.*

33. *Mario Nuzzi,* A Vase of Flowers on its Side, *84x157 cm. Museo del Prado, Madrid.*

34. *Michele Pace, called Michelangelo da Campidoglio,* Flowers, Fruit and Animals in a Park, *96x132 cm. Museo Fesch, Ajaccio.*

35. *Michele Pace, called Michelangelo da Campidoglio,* Fruit and Animals in a Park, *50x65 cm. Ca' d'Oro, Venice.*

36. *Paolo Porpora,* Still Life, *36x64 cm. Banco di Napoli Collection, Museo Nazionale di Capodimonte, Naples.*

28

31

34

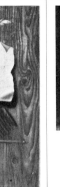

29

32

35

30

33

36

37. *Paolo Porpora,* Still Life, *36x64 cm. Banco di Napoli Collection, Museo Nazionale di Capodimonte, Naples.*

38. *Giovanni Battista Recco,* A Basket of Lobsters, *96x77 cm., signed* Gio Batta Recco. *Private Collection.*

39. *Giuseppe Recco,* Still Life with a Collection of Glasses, *signed* Gios. Recco. *Narodowe Muzeum, Warsaw.*

40. *Giuseppe Recco,* Marine Still Life, *176x230 cm., signed and dated* Gios. Recco 1666. *Private Collection, Naples.*

41. *Giuseppe Recco,* A Monumental Vase of Flowers, *259x206 cm., signed and dated* EQVES RECCVS 1683. *Marquess of Exeter, Burghley House.*

42. *Giuseppe Recco,* Still Life with Game, *92x118 cm., signed* G. R.. *Location unknown.*

43. *Giuseppe Recco,* Study for a Still Life of Fish, *104x127 cm., drawing. Causa Collection, Naples.*

44. *Nicola Maria Recco,* Still Life with Fish, *76x10 cm., signed* Nic. Recco. *Private Collection.*

45. *Giovan Battista Ruoppolo,* Still Life with Flowers and Plants, *106x84 cm., signed* GBruop.lo *Ashmolean Museum, Oxford.*

37

40

43

38

41

44

39

42

45

. *Giuseppe Ruoppolo,* Still Life with Citrus Fruits, x101 cm., *signed* Ruoppoli. *Galleria Gasparrini, me.*

. *Giovanni Paolo Spadino,* Still Life with a Parrot, 2x94 cm. *Museo Fesch, Ajaccio.*

. *Ignaz Stern,* Roses and other Flowers in a ulpted Vase, with Putti, *102x140 cm., signed and ed* I. S. Roma 1743. *Formerly Christie's, New rk, November 14, 1979, no. 181.*

49. *Simone del Tintore,* Still Life with Figures and Animals, *207x545 cm. Private Collection.*

50. *Simone del Tintore,* Still Life with a Basket of Fruit, *72x133 cm., signed* S. T. *Musei Civici del Castello Sforzesco, Milan.*

51. *Giovanni Domenico Valentino,* Kitchen Scene, *121x170 cm., signed* GDVR. *Location unknown.*

52. *Giovanni Domenico Valentino,* Kitchen Scene with Cat, *121x170 cm., signed* GDVR. *Location unknown.*

53. *Agostino Verrocchi,* Still Life, *94x131 cm., signed* AVGVSTINVS VERROCHIVS E. *Galleria Gasparrini, Rome.*

46

49

52

47

50

53

48

51

bromson, M. C. *Painting in Rome during the Papacy of Clement VIII (1592-1605)*. New York, 1981.

ngelini, L. *I Baschenis pittori bergamaschi*. Bergamo, 1946.

"Evaristo Baschenis" in *Dizionario Biografico degli Italiani*. 7. Rome, 965, pp. 61-62.

rcangeli, F. "Il fratello del Guercino." *Arte antica e moderna*, 1961, pp. 25-343.

"Nature morte di Giuseppe Maria Crespi." *Paragone*, no. 149, 1962, pp. 20-32.

rfelli, A., ed. *Carlo Cesare Malvasia, Vite di Pittore Bolognesi (Appunti nediti)*. Bologna, 1961.

risi, F. *Felice Boselli*. Rome, 1973.

aglione, G. *Le vite de' pittori, scultori, architetti ed intagliatori, dal ontificato di Gregorio XIII dal 1572, fino a' tempi di Papa Urbano VIII el 1642*. Rome, 1642. [*ed. 1649*].

aldini, U. "Cristoforo Monari e la natura morte emiliana." *Antichità iva*, III, nos. 9-10, 1964, pp. 64-69.

aldinucci, F. *Notizie de' professori del disegno da Cimabue in qua*. 6 ols. Florence, 1681, 5 vols., Florence, 1845. with Appendix 2 vols., Florence, 1975.

aldinucci, F. S. *Vite di Artisti dei Secoli XVII-XVIII. Prima Edizione ntegrale del Codice Palatino 565*, Matteoli, A., ed. Rome, 1975.

argellesi, G. "Un altro pittore di nature morte casalinghe Arcangelo Resani (Roma 1670-1740 ca.)." *Emporium*, 133, 1961, pp. 153-157.

aroni, C. "Di alcuni sviluppi della pittura Cremonese dal manierismo al barocco. Il Panfilo Nuvolone." *Emporium*, 103, 1946, pp. 233-241.

attisti, E. "Profilo del Gobbo dei Carracci." *Commentari*, 4, 1954, pp. 290-302.

aumgart, F. "Die Caravaggio - Forschung Seit 1943" in *Zeitschrift für Kunstgeschichte*, 1954, pp. 196-203.

ellori, G. P. *Le vite de' pittori scultori ed architetti moderni*. Rome, 672. [*ed. 1976 Torino*].

enedict, C. "Osias Beert." *L'amour de l'art*, 1938.

erenson, B. *Del Caravaggio delle sue incongruenze e della sua fama*. Florence, 1951.

ergamo, Galleria Lorenzelli. *Evaristo Baschenis (1607-1677)*. Exh. at., 1965.

ergström, I. *Dutch Still-Life Painting in the Seventeenth Century*. New York, 1956.

Maestros Espanoles de Bodegones y Floreros del Siglo XVII. Madrid, 1970.

Natura in Posa. Bergamo, 1971.

ertolotti, A. *Artisti lombardi a Roma nei secoli XV, XVI e XVII*. Milan, 881.

iancale, M. "Evaristo Baschenis bergamasco dipintore degli antichi liuti taliane." *L'Arte*. XV, 1912, pp. 321-344.

odart, D. *Les Peintres des Pays-Bas Méridionaux et de la Principauté de Liège à Rome au XVIIe Siècle*. vol. I. Brussels-Rome, 1970, pp. 483ff.

"Abraham Brueghel et la Nature Morte Romaine du XVIIème Siècle" in *Colloqui del Sodalizio tra Studiosi dell'Arte*. Rome, Ser. 2, No. 4, 1973-74, pp. 138-142.

ologna, F. *Natura in Posa*. Exh. cat., Galleria Lorenzelli, Bergamo, 1968.

ologna, Palazzi del Podesta e di Re Enzo. *L'Arte del Settecento Emiliano, La pittura, L'Accademia Clementina*. Exh. cat., 1979.

oom, F. H. "An early flower piece by Jacques de Gheyn II." *Simiolus*, 8, 1975/76, pp. 195-198.

ordeaux, Galerie des Beaux-Arts. *L'art et la musique*. Exh. cat., 1969.

La nature morte de Brueghel à Soutine. Exh. cat., 1978.

orea, E. "Farelli e Fardella: Questioni Relative a Due Pittori Meridionali in Toscana" in *Scritti di Storia dell'arte in onore di Ugo Procacci*, Milan, vol. 2, pp. 554-556.

Caravaggio e Caravaggeschi nelle gallerie di Firenze. Exh. cat., Palazzo Pitti, Florence, 1970.

Pittori Bolognesi del seicento nelle gallerie di Firenze. Exh. cat., Uffizi, Florence, 1975.

Borenius, T. "Two Still Life Paintings by Murillo." *The Burlington Magazine*, XLVIII, 1926, pp. 502ff.

Borroni, S. F. "Le esposizioni d'arte a Firenze 1674-1767." *Mitteilungen des Kunsthistorisches Instituts in Florenz*. XVIII. 1974, pp. 1-166.

Bottari, G. *Raccolta di lettere sulla Pittura*. Rome, 1754/1783.

Bottari, G./Ticozzi, S. *Raccolta di lettere sulla pittura, scultura ed architettura...* Milan, 1822-1825.

Bottari, S. "Un'opera di Pietro Paolo Bonzi." *Arte antica e moderna*, no. 11, 1960, pp. 294-295.

"Due 'nature morte' dell'Empoli." *Arte antica e moderna*, no. 9, 1960 (2), pp. 75-76.

"Appunti sui Recco." *Arte antica e moderna*, 1961, pp. 354-361.

"Fede Galizia." *Arte antica e moderna*, no. 24, 1963, pp. 309-318.

"Una traccia per Luca Forte e il primo tempo della 'natura morta' a Napoli." *Arte antica e moderna*, no. 23, 1963 (2), pp. 242-246.

"Un ipotesi per Aniello Falcone." *Arte antica e moderna*. nos. 34-36, 1966, pp. 141-143.

Briganti, G. "Michelangelo Cerquozzi pittore di nature morte." *Paragone*, no. 53, 1954, pp. 47-52.

"Cristoforo Munari." *Paragone*, no. 55, 1954 (2), pp. 40-42.

Pietro da Cortona. Florence, 1962.

Bruno G., et. al. *La Pittura a Genova e in Liguria dal Seicento al primo Novecento*. Genoa, 1971.

Buffa, S., ed. *The Illustrated Bartsch (XVII, Part I)*. 34, New York, 1982.

Campori, G. *Gli artisti italiani e stranieri negli stati estensi*. Modena, 1855.

Lettere artistiche inedite. Modena, 1866.

Raccolta di cataloghi ed inventarii inediti. Modena, 1870.

Castelnovi, G. V., *La Galleria Rizzi a Sestri Levante*, Associazione fra le Casse di Risparmio Italiane. 1972.

"La pittura nella prima metà del Seicento" in *La Pittura a Genova dal Seicento al primo Novecento*. II, Genoa, 1971.

Causa, R. "Paolo Porpora e il primo tempo della 'natura morta' napoletana." *Paragone*, no. 15, 1951, pp. 31-33.

"Un avvio per Giacomo Recco." *Arte antica e moderna*, 1961, pp. 344-353.

"Luca Forte e il primo tempo della natura morta napoletana." *Paragone*, no. 145, 1962, pp. 41-48.

La pittura del seicento a Napoli dal naturalismo al barocco. Naples, 1972.

"La nature morte italienne au XVIIe Siècle en Italie" in *La nature morte de Breughel à Soutine*, Exh. cat., Galerie des Beaux Arts, Bordeaux, 1978, pp. 39-48.

Cavestany, J. *Exposicion de Floreros y Bodegones en la Pintura Española*. Exh. cat., Palacio de la Biblioteca Nacional, Madrid, 1941.

Chiarini, M. "Il maestro 'G.D.V.'." *Paragone*, no. 295, 1974, pp. 73-74.

"I Quadri della Collezione del Principe Ferdinando di Toscana." *Paragone*, no. 301, 1975, pp. 57-98; no. 303, 1975, pp. 53-88.

Ciardi, R. P. *Giovan Ambrogio Figino*. Florence, 1968.

Cinotti, M., ed. *Immagine del Caravaggio*. Exh. cat., Milan, 1973.

Cipriani, A. "Giovanna Garzoni, Miniatrice" in *Il Seicento/Documenti e Interpretazione*. Ricerche di Storia dell'Arte, 1-2, 1976, pp. 241-254.

Colasanti, A. *Volte e Soffitti Italiani*. Milan, 1915.

Colding, T. H. *Aspects of Miniature Painting: Its Origins and Development*. Copenhagen, 1953.

Cologne, *Stilleben-Natura Morta im Wallraf-Richartz-Museum und im Museum Ludwig*. Exh. cat., 1980.

Colonna, F. "Inventario dei Quadri di Casa Colonna." *Napoli Nobilissima*, IV, 1895, pp. 29-32.

Cooney, J. P. *L'opera completa di Annibale Carracci*. Milan, 1976.

Corbara, A. "Tre nature morte di Arcangelo Resani." *Paragone*, no. 183,

1965, pp. 52-55.

Craig, K. "Pieter Aertsen." *Oud Holland.* 1982.

Crespi, L. *Felsina Pittrice Vite de' Pittori Bolognesi,* III, *supplemento all'Opera del Malvasia.* Rome, 1769 [ed. 1970 Bologna].

Curtis, C. B. *Velazquez and Murillo,* London, 1883.

D'Addosio, G. B. "Documenti inediti di artisti napoletani del XVI e XVII secolo." *Archivio storico per le province Napoletane,* 38, 1913.

D'Ancona, M. Levi. *The Garden of the Renaissance Botanical Symbolism in Italian Painting.* Florence, 1977.

Dacos, N. "Il trastullo di Raffaello." *Paragone,* 1968, pp. 3-29.

Dal Pozzo, B. *Le vite de' pittori, degli scultori et architetti veronesi.* Verona, 1718.

Daniels, J. *L'opera completa di Sebastiano Ricci.* Milan, 1976.
Sebastiano Ricci. Hove, England, 1976.

De Dominici, B. *Vite de' pittori, scultori ed architetti napoletani.* 3 vols. Naples, 1742/43.

De Jongh, E. "Grape Symbolism in Paintings of the 16th and 17th Centuries." *Simiolus,* vol. 7, 1974, pp. 166-191.

de Juliis, G. "Appunti su una Quadreria Fiorentina: La Collezione dei Marchesi Riccardi." *Paragone.* no. 375, 1981, pp. 57-92.

Della Pergola, P. *Galleria Borghese — I Dipinti.* II. Rome, 1959.

Del Bravo, C. "Una 'figura con natura morta' del seicento toscano." *Arte antica e moderna,* 1961, pp. 322-324.

De Logu, G. *Pittori Minori Liguri Lombardi Piemontesi del Seicento e del Settecento.* Venice, 1931.
"Cristoforo Monari o Monaricco." *Emporium.* CXXI. 1955, pp. 249-258.
"Un nuovo piccolo maestro: Bartolomeo Bimbi." *Emporium.* LXVI. 1960, pp. 59-66.
Natura Morta Italiana, Bergamo, 1962.

De Rinaldis, A. "D'Arpino e Caravaggio." *Bollettino d'Arte.* June, 1936, pp. 577-580.

De Tolnay, C. "Postilla sulle origini della natura morta moderna." *Rivista d'Arte.* 1961/62, pp. 3-10.

Detroit, Detroit Institute of Arts. *Art in Italy: 1600-1700.* Exh. cat., 1965.
The Twilight of the Medici. Exh. cat., 1974.

De Vries, S. "Jacopo Chimenti da Empoli." *Rivista d'Arte.* 1933. pp. 329-339.

Diaz Padrón, M. *Museo del Prado Catálogo de Pinturas I Escuela Flamenca Siglo XVII.* Madrid, 1975.

Dumont, C. *Francesco Salviati au Palais Sacchetti de Rome et la décoration murale italienne (1520-1560).* Rome, 1973.

Emiliani, A. *La Pinacoteca Nazionale di Bologna.* Bologna, 1967.

Emmens, J. A. "'Einsaber is nötig' — Zur Inhalt und Bedeutung von Markt — und Küchenstücken des 16. Jahrhunderts" in *Album Amicorum J. G. van Gelder.* The Hague, 1973, pp. 93-101.

Ertz, K. *Jan Brueghel der Ältere Die Gemälde.* Cologne, 1979.

Exeter, Marchioness of. *Catalogue of Pictures at Burghley House Northamptonshire.* 1954.

Faldi, I. "I dipinti chigiani di Michele e Giovan Battista Pace." *Arte antica e moderna.* nos. 34-36, 1966, pp. 144-150.

Faré, M. *Le Grand Siècle de la Nature Morte en France.* Paris, 1974.

Ferrari, O. and G. Scavizzi. *Luca Giordano.* 3 vols. Naples, 1966.

Finarte. Exh. cat. no. 4., Milan, 1963.

Florence, Palazzo Pitti. *La mostra della pittura italiana del sei e settecento in palazzo Pitti.* Exh. cat., 1922.
Artisti alla Corte Granducale. Exh. cat., 1969.

Florence, Gabinetto Disegni e Stampi degli Uffizi. *Mostra di Disegni di Jacopo Ligozzi.* Exh. cat., 1961.

Freedberg, S. J. *Painting in Italy 1500 to 1600.* Rev. ed. Baltimore, Md., 1975.

Friedlaender, W. *Caravaggio Studies.* Princeton, N. J., 1974.

Frommel, C. L. "Caravaggios Frühwerk und der Kardinal Francesco Maria del Monte." *Storia dell'Arte.* 1971/72, pp. 5-52.

G. B. Castiglione. Fonti per la storia della pittura, II. Genoa, 1973.
Fonti per la storia della pittura, III. Monzambano, 1975.

Garas, K. "The Ludovisi Collection of Pictures in 1633/(- -) - II." *The Burlington Magazine,* CIX, 1967, pp. 339-349.

Geddo, A. *Evaristo Baschenis.* Bergamo, 1965.

Geneva, Musée d'art et d'histoire, *Art Venitien en Suisse et au Liechtenstein.* Exh. cat., 1978.

Genoa, Palazzo Bianco. *Pittori Genovesi a Genova nel '600 e nel '700.* Exh. cat., 1969.

Ghidiglia Quintavalle, A. *Cristoforo Munari e la natura morta Emiliana* Exh. cat., Parma, 1964.

Gli Uffizi, Catalogo Generale. Florence, 1979/80.

Gombosi, G. *Moretto da Brescia.* Basel, 1943.

Gombrich, E. H. *Meditations on a Hobby Horse.* London, 1978.

Graf. D. and E. Schleier "Guglielmo Cortese und Abraham Brueghel." *Pantheon.* January 1974, pp. 46-57.

Il Grechetto a Mantova. Fonti per la storia della pittura, I. Genoa, 1971.

Gregori, M. "Nuove schede per la natura morta italiana." *Antichità viva* IV, no. 1, 1965, pp. 11-18.
70 pitture e sculture del '600 e '700 fiorentino. Exh. cat., Palazzo Strozz Florence, 1965 (2).
"Notizie su Agostino Verrocchi un'ipotesi per Giovanni Battista Crescenzi." *Paragone,* no. 275, 1973, pp. 36-56.

Grosso, O. "Anton Maria Vassallo e la pittura di animali nei primi del '600 a Genova." *Dedalo,* III, 1923, pp. 502-522.

Hartford, Wadsworth Atheneum. *Harvest of Plenty.* Exh. cat., 1963.

Harris, A. S. and L. Nochlin. *Women Artists 1550-1950.* New York, 1979.

Haskell, F. *Patrons and Painters.* London, 1963.

Hess, J. "Tassi, Bonzi e Cortona a Palazzo Mattei." *Commentari,* no. 4, 1954, pp. 303-315.

Hoogewerff, G. J. "Nature morte italiane del Seicento e del Settecento." *Dedalo,* IV, 1924, pp. 599-624, 710-730.
"Abramo Breughel e Niccolino van Houbraken pittori di fiori in Italia." *Dedalo,* XI, 1930/31, pp. 482-494.
De Bentvueghels. s'Gravenhage, 1952.

Kuznetzov, I. *West European Still-Life Painting.* Leningrad, 1966.

L'Accademia Nazionale di S. Luca. Rome, 1974.

La Fondazione Roberto Longhi a Firenze. Milan, 1980.

"La natura morta a Napoli." *Antichità viva,* III, nos. 7-8, 1964, pp. 59-68.

Lavin, M. A. *Seventeenth-Century Barberini Documents and Inventorie. of Art.* New York, 1975.

London, Matthiesen Fine Art Ltd. *Important Italian Baroque Paintings 1600-1700.* Exh. cat., 1981.

London, Royal Academy of Arts. *Paintings in Naples 1606-1705 from Caravaggio to Giordano.* Exh. cat., 1982.

Longhi, R. "Quesiti Caravaggeschi. II." *Pinacotheca,* 1928/29, pp. 258-320.
"Ultimi studi sul Caravaggio." *I proporzioni,* I, 1943, pp. 5-63.
"Un momento importante nella storia della 'natura morta'." *Paragone,* no. 1, 1950, pp. 34-39.
"La mostra della natura morta all'Orangerie." *Paragone,* no. 33, 1952, pp. 46-52.
"Anche Ambrogio Figino sulla soglia della 'natura morta'." *Paragone,* no. 209, 1967, pp. 18ff.
Caravaggio. Rome, 1968 [ed. 1982]).

Lopez-Navio, J. "La gran colección de pinturas del Marqués de

.eganés." *Analecta Calasanctrava,* 8, 1962, pp. 260-330.

cCorquodale, C. *Painting in Florence 1600-1700.* Exh. cat., Royal
Academy of Arts, London, 1979.

adrid, Museo del Prado. *Pintura Italiana del Siglo XVII.* Exh. cat.,
970.

adrid, Museo del Prado. *El Arte europeo en la Corte de España durante
.l siglo XVIII.* Exh. cat., 1979/80.

alaguzzi Valeri, F. *Catalogo della Pinacoteca di Brera.* Bergamo, 1908.

alvasia, C. C. *Felsina pittrice, vite de' pittori bolognesi,* Bologna, 1678;
Zanotti ed., 1841.

ancini, A. *Considerazioni sulla pittura.* Edited by A. Marucchi and L.
Salerno. 2 vols. Rome, 1956/57.

anning, R. L. *Neapolitan Masters.* Exh. cat., Finch College Museum of
Art, New York, 1962.

anning, R. L. and B. Suida Manning. *Genoese Masters: Cambiaso to
Magnasco 1550-1750.* Exh. cat., Dayton Ohio Art Institute, 1962.

arabottini Marabotti, A. "Il 'naturalismo' di Pietro Paolini" in *Scritti
.i Storia dell'Arte in Onore di Mario Salmi.* I. Rome, 1963, pp. 307-324.

arangoni, M. "Due 'nature morte' di Jacopo da Empoli." *Bollettino
.'Arte.* 1922/23, p. 480.

arini, M. *Io Michelangelo da Caravaggio.* Rome. 1974.

arrini, O. *Serie di ritratti originali di celebri pittori dipinti di propria
.iano.* Firenze, 1764.

artin, J. R. *Baroque.* New York, 1977.

asini, A. *Bologna Perlustrata.* Bologna, 1666.

ayer, A. L. *Monatschrift für Kunstwissenschaft,* VIII, 1915.

eloni Trkulja, Silvia. "Bimbi, Bartolomeo" in *Dizionario Biografico
.egli Italiani,* 10, Rome, 1968, p. 480.

"Leopoldo de' Medici Collezionista." *Paragone,* no. 307, 1975, pp.
5-38.

.l Servizio del Granduca. Exh. cat., Palazzo Pitti, Florence, 1980.

.ilan, Galleria Phillippe Daverio. *Natura Morta in Italia.* Exh. cat.,
.981.

.odena, Palazzo dei Musei. *Mostra di Opere Restaurate secoli XIV-XIX.*
.xh. cat., 1980/81.

.oir, A. *The Italian Followers of Caravaggio.* Cambridge, Mass., 1967.

Caravaggio and His Copyists. New York, 1976.

.ongitore, A. *Memorie dei Pittori, Scultori, Architetti, Artefici in Cera
.iciliani.* Edited by E. Natoli. Palermo, 1977.

.ortari, L. *Bernardo Strozzi.* Rome, 1966.

.ünster, Westfälisches Landesmuseum für Kunst und Kulturgeschichte,
.nd Baden-Baden, Staatliche Kunsthalle. *Stilleben in Europa.* Exh. cat.,
.980.

.antes, Musée des Beaux-Arts. *Supplément au Catalogue des Peintures
.953-1960.* Nantes, 1960.

.aples, Palazzo Reale. *La Natura Morta Italiana.* Exh. cat., 1964.

.Neapolitan museums]. *Civiltà del '700 a Napoli 1734-1799.* Exh. cat. 2
.ols. 1979/80.

.atura in Posa. Milan, 1977.

.eilson, N. W. "A Drawing by Panfilo Nuvolone." *The Burlington
Magazine,* 111, April 1969, pp. 219-220.

.icolson, B. and C. Wright. *Georges de la Tour.* London, 1974.

.icolson, B. *The International Caravaggesque Movement.* Oxford, 1979.

.ota de' Quadri che sono esposti per la festa di S. Luca dagli Accademici
.el Disegno nella loro Capella posta nel Chiostro del Monastero de'
.adri della SS. Nonziata di Firenze l'Anno 1706.

.ota de' Quadri e Opere di Scultura esposti per la festa di S. Luca dagli
.ccademici del Disegno nella loro Capella e nel Chiostro secondo del
.onvento de' PP. della SS. Nonziata di Firenze l'Anno 1729.

.jetti, U., L. Dami and N. Tarchiani. *La pittura italiana del seicento e del
.ettecento alla mostra di palazzo Pitti.* Milan and Rome, 1924.

Orbaan, J. A. F. "Virtuosi al Pantheon. Archivalische Beiträge zur
Römischen Kunstgeschichte." *Repertorium für Kunstwissenschaft,*
XXXVII, 1959, pp. 3-52.

Orlandi, P. A. *L'Abecedario Pittorico.* Naples, 1733.

Ortolani, S. *La pittura napoletana dal sei all'ottocento.* Exh. cat..
Castelnuovo, Naples, 1938.

Ostrow, S. *Baroque Painting. Italy and her Influence.* Exh. cat.,
Providence, Rhode Island, 1968.

Ottani Cavina, A. *Carlo Saraceni.* Milan, 1968.

Ottani Cavina, A. "On the Theme of Landscape - II: Elsheimer and
Galileo." *The Burlington Magazine.* 128, March 1976, pp. 139-144.

Oxford, Ashmolean Museum. *Catalogue of the Collection of Dutch and
Flemish Still-Life Pictures Bequeathed by Daisy Linda Ward.* 1950.

Pallucchini, R. *La Galleria Estense di Modena.* Rome, 1945.

Parma, Pinacoteca. *Arte in Emilia.* Exh. cat., 1960/61.

Arte in Emilia II. Exh. cat., 1962.

Paris, Musée du Louvre. *Dessins baroques florentins du Musée du
Louvre.* Exh. cat., 1981/82.

Pascoli, L. *Vite de' pittori, scultori e d'architetti moderni.* 2 vols. Rome,
1730-1736.

Passeri, G. B. *Vite dei pittori, scultori ed architetti che anno lavorato in
Roma morti dal 1641 al 1673.* Edited by J. Hess. Leipzig and Vienna,
1934.

Pepper, D. S. "Annibale Carracci ritrattista." *Arte illustrata.* 6, 1973,
pp. 127-137.

Percy, A. *Giovanni Benedetto Castiglione: Master Draughtsman of the
Italian Baroque.* Exh. cat., Philadelphia Museum of Art, Philadelphia,
Pa., 1971.

Perez Sanchez, A. E. *Pintura Italiana del S. XVII in España.* Madrid,
1965.

Perotti, A. *I pittori Campi da Cremona.* Milan, 1932.

Pio, N. *Le vite di pittori scultori et architetti.* Edited by C. Enggass and R.
Enggass. Vatican City, 1977.

Pope-Hennessy, J. *Luca della Robbia.* Ithaca, New York, 1980.

Posner, D. "Caravaggio's Homo-Erotic Early Works." *Art Quarterly.* 34,
1971, pp. 301-324.

Prohaska, W. "Untersuchungen zur 'Rosenkranzmadonna'
Caravaggios." *Jahrbuch der Kunsthistorischen Sammlungen in Wien,*
76, 1980, pp. 111-132.

Prota-Giurleo, U. *Pittori Napoletani del Seicento.* Naples, 1950.

Ravelli, L. *Polidoro Caldara da Caravaggio.* "Monumenta
Bergomensia." XLVIII, 1978.

Rearick, W. R. "Jacopo Bassano's Later Genre Paintings." *The
Burlington Magazine,* 110, 1968, pp. 241-249.

Riccomini, E. "Pier Francesco Cittadini." *Arte antica e moderna,* 1961,
pp. 362-373.

ed., *Pittura Italiana del Settecento.* Exh. cat., Soprintendenza alle
Gallerie di Bologna, Leningrad, Moscow, Warsaw, 1974.

Riewarts, T. and P. Pieper. *Die Maler tom Ring.* Munich, 1955.

Ripa, C. *Iconologia.* Padua, 1611.

Roli, R. "Due ritratti di Carlo Magini." *Arte antica e moderna,* no. 33,
1966, pp. 88-90.

Pittura Bolognese 1650-1800 dal Cignani ai Gandolfi. Bologna, 1977.

Rome, Palazzo delle Esposizioni. *Il seicento europeo.* Exh. cat., 1956/57.

Rosci, M. *Baschenis Bettera & Co.,* Milan, 1971.

"Italia" in *Natura in posa, La Grande Stagione della Natura Morta,*
Milan, 1977, pp. 83-112.

Rosenberg, P. *France in the Golden Age: Seventeenth Century Paintings
in American Collections.* Exh. cat., New York, 1982.

Rossi, F. *Accademia Carrara Bergamo. Catalogo dei dipinti,* Bergamo,
1979.

Röttgen, H. *Il Caravaggio ricerche e interpretazioni.* Rome, 1974.

Rubin, W. *Cezanne — The Late Work,* New York, 1977.

Rudolph, S. " Carlo Maratti figurista per pittori di nature morte. " *Antichità viva,* XVIII, no. 2, 1979, pp. 12-20.
Ruffo, V. "Galleria Ruffo nel Secolo XVII in Messina." *Bolletino d'Arte,* 1916, pp. 21-64.
Ruotolo, R. " Collezioni e mecenati napoletani del XVII secolo." *Napoli nobilissima,* XII, 1973, pp. 145-153.

Salerno, L. " Di Tommaso Salini, Un Ignorato Caravaggesco. " *Commentari,* 3, 1952, pp. 28-31.
" Precisazioni su Giovanni Lanfranco e su Tommaso Salini," *Commentari,* 1954, pp. 253-255.
" The Picture Gallery of Vincenzo Giustiniani." *The Burlington Magazine,* 1960, pp. 21-26, 93-104, 135-150.
Sandrart, J. *Accademiae nobilissimae Artis pictoriae.* Nuremberg, 1683.
Scaramuccia, L. *Le finezze de' pennelli italiani.* Pavia, 1674.
Schwarz, H. " The Mirror in Art." *The Art Quarterly,* 15, 1952, pp. 97-118.
Schwarz, H. and V. Plagemann. " Eule " in *Reallexikon zur Deutschen Kunstgeschichte,* VI, Munich, 1973, pp. 267-322.
Schwarz, H. *Salzburg und das Salzkammergut,* Salzburg, 4th rev. ed. 1977.
Segal, S. *A Flowery Past.* Exh. cat., Amsterdam, 1982.
Sestieri, E. " Due Luca Forte." *Commentari,* 23, 1972, p. 376f.
Shapley, F. R. *Paintings from the Samuel H. Kress Collection: Italian Schools XVI-XVIII Century.* London, 1973.
Catalogue of the Italian Paintings. National Gallery of Art, Washington, D.C., 1979.
Soprani, R. *Le vite de' pittori... Genovesi.* Genoa, 1674.
Soprani, R. and C. G. Ratti. *Vite de' pittori, scultori, ed architetti genovesi.* Genoa, 1769.
Spear, R. E. *Caravaggio and His Followers.* Rev. ed. New York, 1975.
Spike, J. T. *Italian Baroque Paintings from New York Private Collections.* Exh. cat., Princeton, New Jersey, 1980.
Spinosa, N., ed. *Le arti figurative a Napoli nel settecento. Naples, 1979.*
The State Hermitage: West-European Painting. Vol. 1. Moscow, 1957.
Sterling, C. *La Nature morte de l'antiquité à nos jours.* Musée de l'Orangerie. Exh. cat., Paris, 1952.
Still Life Painting from Antiquity to the Twentieth Century. 1st English ed. 1959; 2nd rev. ed. 1981.
Strinati, C. *Quadri Romani tra '500 e '600 opere restaurate e da restaurare.* Exh. cat., Palazzo Venezia. Rome, 1979.

Tassi, F. M. *Vite de' pittori, scultori e architetti Bergamaschi.* 1793.
Thieme-Becker Künstlerlexicon, XXVIII, Leipzig, 1933.
Titi, F. *Studio di pittura, scoltura et architettura nelle chiese di Roma.* Rome, 1674.
Ammaestramento... di pittura, scoltura et architettura nelle chiese di Roma. Rome, 1686.
Tomory, P. *Catalogue of the Italian Paintings before 1800. The John & Mable Ringling Museum of Art,* Sarasota, 1976.
Torres Martin, R. *Blas de Ledesma y el Bodegon Español.* Madrid, 1978.
Torriti, P. " La natura morta e il paesaggio " in *La Pittura a Genova dal Seicento al primo Novecento.* II, Genoa, 1971.

Urrea Fernandez, J. *La Pintura Italiana del Siglo XVIII en España.* Valladolid, 1977.

Valsecchi, M. ed. *Il seicento lombardo, catalogo dei dipinti e delle sculture.* Exh. cat., Palazzo Reale, Milan, 1973.
Van der Meer, J. H. and H. Friedemann. " Strumenti musicali in un quadro attribuito a Munari." *Antichità viva,* X, no. 6, 1971, pp. 12-16.
Veca, A. *Inganno & Realtà.* Exh. cat. Bergamo, 1980.
Vanitas. Exh. cat. Bergamo, 1981.
Venezia, Palazzo Ducale. *I Fiamminghi e l'Italia.* Exh. cat., 1951.
Venturi, A. " Affreschi nella delizia estense di Sassuolo." *L'Arte,* XX, 1917, pp. 67-69, 71, 79, 82.
Storia dell'arte italiana. Milan, 1933.
Vesme, A. Baudi di. *La Regia Pinacoteca di Torino* in *Le Gallerie Nazionali Italiane,* anno III, Rome, 1897.
Volpe, C. " Annotazioni sulla Mostra Caravaggesca di Cleveland. " *Paragone,* no. 263, 1972, pp. 50-76.
Mostra di dipinti dal XIV al XVIII secolo. Finarte, no. 9, Milan, 1972 (2).

Waterhouse, E. *Italian Baroque Painting.* 2nd ed. London, 1969.
Roman Baroque Painting. Oxford, 1976.
Wind, B. " Vincenzo Campi and Hans Fugger: A Peep at Late Cinquecento Bawdy Humor." *Arte Lombarda,* 47/48, 1977, pp. 108-114.
Wittkower, R. *Art and Architecture in Italy 1600 to 1750.* 3rd rev. ed. Baltimore, Md., 1973.

Zamboni, S. " Vincenzo Campi." *Arte antica e moderna,* no. 30, 1965, pp. 124-147.
Zeri, F. " Giuseppe Recco una natura morta giovanile." *Paragone,* III, no. 33, 1950, pp. 37-38.
La galleria Pallavicini in Roma. Florence, 1959.
" Sull'esecuzione di ' natura morte' nella bottega del Cavalier d'Arpino e sulla presenza ivi del giovane Caravaggio " in *Diari di Lavoro 2.* Turin 1976, pp. 92-103.
" Nota a Tommaso Salini " in *Diari di Lavoro 2.* Turin, 1976 (2), pp. 104-108.
Italian Paintings in the Walters Art Gallery. Baltimore, Md., 1976 (3).

gliardi Collection, Bergamo   Figs. 24, 25, 26.
rchivi Alinari, Florence   Figs. 12, 13.
en Brown, Milwaukee   R.P. 21.
rudence Cumming Ass. Ltd., London   Exh. nos. 31, 33.
ourtauld Institute of Art, London   R.P. 41.
tudio Da Re, Bergamo   Pl. 2; R.P. 11.
etroit Institute of Art, Detroit   Fig. 15.
otofast, Bologna   Fig. 20.
oto Paltronieri, Lugano   Exh. nos. 3, 4, 5, 6, 13, 14, 24, 45, 46; fig. 5.
alleria degli Uffizi, Florence   Pl. 3; Exh. nos. 18, 37.
alleria Doria Pamphilj, Rome   Pl. 4.
alleria Gasparrini, Rome   R.P. 46, 53.
alleria Lorenzelli, Bergamo   Fig. 6; R.P. 13.
tituto Centrale per il Catalogo e la Documentazione, Roma   Fig. 11.
iechtenstein Collection, Vaduz   Pl. 5.
os Angeles County Museum, Los Angeles   Exh. no. 43.
runo Meissner, Zurich   Exh. no. 23; fig. 18; R.P. 18.
enil Foundation, Houston   R.P. 24.
useo del Prado, Madrid   R.P. 6, 8, 9, 32, 33.
useo Rizzi, Sestri Levante   Fig. 29.
ational Gallery of Art, Washington   Exh. nos. 11, 35.
ationalmuseum, Stockholm   R.P. 2.
edicini, Naples   Exh. nos. 15, 16, 27, 28, 29, 30, 32, 40, 41, 42.
inacoteca Ambrosiana, Milan   Pl. 1.
inacoteca Civica, Faenza   Exh. no. 36, 44.
ijksmuseum-Stichting, Amsterdam   Fig. 10.
hn and Mable Ringling Museum of Art, Sarasota   Exh. no. 17.
ammlung Thyssen-Bornemisza, Lugano   Exh. no. 12.
cala, Florence   Exh. nos. 8, 9, 19, 20, 21, 22, 38.
oprintendenza per i Beni Artistici e Storici delle provincie di Firenze e
istoia, Florence   Figs. 21, 22, 23, 30, 31, 34; R.P. 5, 12, 19, 23.
oprintendenza per i Beni Artistici e Storici, Pinacoteca di Brera,
ilan   Figs. 1, 2.
oprintendenza ai Beni Artistici e Storici, Naples   R.P. 37, 43.
oprintendenza per i Beni Artistici e Storici di Modena e Reggio Emilia,
lodena   Exh. no. 26.
ario Tornone, Milan   Exh. nos. 1, 2.
niversity of Oxford, Ashmolean Museum, Oxford   R.P. 45.
. Villani e figli, Bologna   Figs. 7, 8, 19, 27, 28, 32; R.P. 4, 7, 30, 31, 34,
5, 36, 39, 40, 47, 50.
Vadsworth Atheneum, Hartford   Exh. no. 10; R.P. 3.